Juniper Networking Technologies

Day One: vMX Up and Running

By Matt Dinham

Published by Juniper Networks Books
Author: Matt Dinham
Technical Reviewers: Paul Abbott, Peter Head, Said van de Klundert, David Roy, Simon Zhong
Editor in Chief: Patrick Ames
Copyeditor and Proofer: Nancy Koerbel
J-Net Community Manager: Julie Wider

ISBN: 978-1-941441-35-0 (print)
Printed in the USA by Vervante Corporation.
ISBN: 978-1-941441-36-7 (ebook)

Version History: v1, March 2016
2 3 4 5 6 7 8 9 10

About the Author
Matt Dinham is an independent consulting Network Engineer/Architect based in the UK, and a Juniper Ambassador. Matt has over 15 years experience working within Enterprise and Service Provider environments (public & private sector), and is certified CCIE #16387 (R&S, SP). Find Matt on Twitter: *@mattdinham*.

Author's Acknowledgments
I would like to thank Patrick for the opportunity to write this book, and for his guidance on writing for the Day One series. I would also like to thank the technical reviewers for looking over my words and offering plenty of encouragement along the way. Finally, thanks to Julie Wider and the Ambassador group for the camaraderie.

This book is available in a variety of formats at: http://www.juniper.net/dayone.

Welcome to Day One

This book is part of a growing library of *Day One* books, produced and published by Juniper Networks Books.

Day One books were conceived to help you get just the information that you need on day one. The series covers Junos OS and Juniper Networks networking essentials with straightforward explanations, step-by-step instructions, and practical examples that are easy to follow.

The *Day One* library also includes a slightly larger and longer suite of *This Week* books, whose concepts and test bed examples are more similar to a weeklong seminar.

You can obtain either series, in multiple formats:

- Download a free PDF edition at http://www.juniper.net/dayone.
- Get the ebook edition for iPhones and iPads from the iTunes Store. Search for Juniper Networks Books.
- Get the ebook edition for any device that runs the Kindle app (Android, Kindle, iPad, PC, or Mac) by opening your device's Kindle app and going to the Kindle Store. Search for Juniper Networks Books.
- Purchase the paper edition at either Vervante Corporation (www.vervante.com) for between $12-$28, depending on page length.

Audience

This *Day One* book is intended for network architects and engineers who are interested in learning about Juniper's Virtual MX router (vMX) and how to get started with implementing vMX.

If you are studying for a Juniper Certification, or are used to working with software from another vendor and are trying out the Junos OS for the first time, this book shows you how to use vMX to build and scale your own lab environment.

The configuration and scenarios are designed so you can test out vMX without having access to a huge amount of lab hardware. Everything shown in this book can be completed on a modest specification laptop.

What You Need to Know Before Reading This Book

Before reading this book, you should be familiar with the basic administrative functions of the Junos operating system, including the ability to work with operational commands and to read, understand, and change Junos configurations. There are several books in the *Day One* library on learning Junos, at http://www.juniper.net/dayone.

This book also makes a few assumptions about you, the reader:

- You have a basic understanding of Internet Protocol version 4, IPv4, and the OSPF and BGP routing protocols.
- You are familiar with the Junos OS operation and configuration.
- You have a basic understanding of Linux System Administration (preferably Ubuntu), and knowledge of the Linux Virtualisation solution KVM.
- You have a basic understanding of MPLS.
- For the lab build you have access to a laptop or desktop with at least 4 x CPU cores and 16-32GB RAM.

What You Will Learn by Reading This Book

- Understand the vMX router and be able to deploy the book's use cases.
- Be familiar with the build, configuration, and deployment of vMX in your lab or production environments.
- Know how to scale an instance of vMX.
- Understand how to license vMX for a lab or production deployment.
- How to troubleshoot vMX installation and deployment issues.

Chapter 1

Introduction to vMX

This *Day One* book goes through the lab setup and configuration of Juniper's vMX, running on Ubuntu's Linux. If you are running VMware there is a chapter at the end of this book to walk you through the build. And in this first chapter you will learn about the architecture of the vMX, which is key to understanding its sizing and licensing models. Let's get going.

What is vMX?

The vMX is a virtual Juniper Networks MX Series router that has been optimized to run as software on x86 servers. Like other physical MX routers, vMX runs the Junos OS, and the Trio chipset has been compiled for x86. This means the sophisticated Layer 2, Layer 2.5, and Layer 3 forwarding features of the Junos OS that work with the physical MX platform are also present on the vMX.

The vMX can be installed on any server hardware of your choice, so long as it is x86-based with an Intel Nehalem or newer generation CPU, and running Linux KVM or VMware.

Although this book focuses on a lab build of vMX 15.1 running on Linux KVM, the VMware release of vMX is also now available. There is a chapter at the end of this book to walk you through the installation of vMX on VMware's ESXi Hypervisor.

Architecture of vMX

As shown in Figure 1.1, the vMX actually consists of two separate VMs – a virtual control plane (VCP) running the Junos OS, and a virtual forwarding plane (VFP) running the virtualized Trio forwarding plane.

To route traffic on vMX, each virtual NIC on the VFP is mapped to a physical NIC, a Linux Bridge, or a VMware vSwitch, based on your configuration. These VFP interfaces are then configured via Junos on the VCP.

As you will see during the labs in this book, it is not a requirement to map a physical NIC to the VFP NIC on vMX. You can build lab topologies that consist of many routers without having to use a physical NIC anywhere in the topology. And of course your more complex topologies can make use of physical NICs and bridges/vSwitches at the same time.

Finally, the physical server contains the physical NICs, CPUs, and memory, and provides the management of a vMX instance via a serial console and an Ethernet management interface.

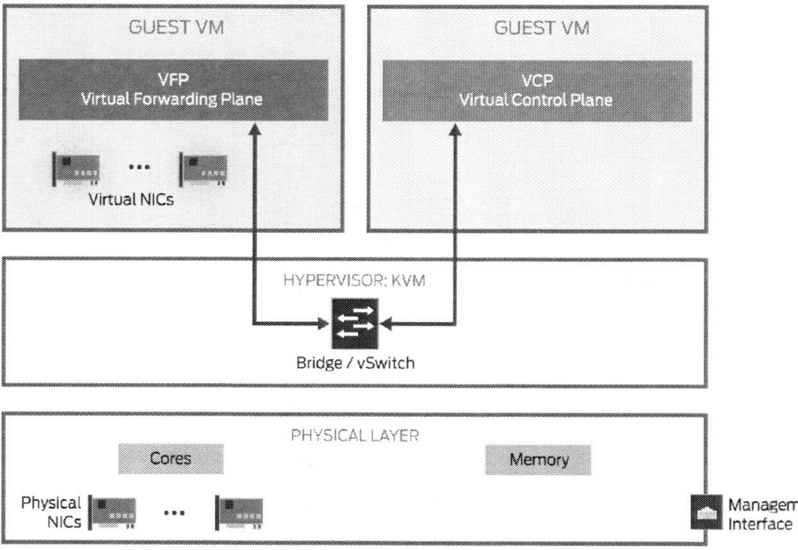

Figure 1.1 vMX Architecture Overview

On Linux, the VMs are managed by an orchestration script provided by Juniper that is used to create, stop, and start the vMX instances. A simple configuration file defines parameters such as memory and vCPUs to allocate to the VCP and VFP. It's not mandatory to use the orchestration script, but doing so will create all the necessary VM configuration for you and provides an easy-to-use mechanism for managing vMX.

The Linux virtualization solution, KVM, is what Juniper uses to spin up the virtual instances of the control and forwarding planes. Multiple instances of vMX can be run on the same physical hardware, and if you desire, other KVM virtual machines can also be running.

That Juniper vMX uses Linux and KVM is no surprise, as they are used on other Juniper products such as the QFX Series, and, of course, more recently with disaggregated Junos OS on the QFX5200 Series.

NOTE If you would like to know more about Junos disaggregation take a look at: http://www.juniper.net/us/en/insights/software-disaggregation/.

Virtual Control Plane (VCP)

The virtual control plane consists of the Junos OS hosted within a virtual machine. As such, all the usual capabilities you are used to seeing on Junos software are available on the vMX. As Junos is based on FreeBSD, the VCP VM is actually running FreeBSD. The VFP is analogous to the RE in the physical MX.

Virtual Forwarding Plane (VFP)

The VFP consists of a virtualized Trio forwarding plane running on Windriver Linux, and is analogous to the FPC in the physical MX. The VFP makes use of the Intel DPDK libraries to optimize user space packet processing. For more information on DPDK see http://www.intel.com/content/www/us/en/intelligent-systems/intel-technology/packet-processing-is-enhanced-with-software-from-intel-dpdk.html.

The DPDK is designed for fast packet processing and low latency. For the lab, or for throughputs of up to 100Mbps, a lite mode is available. For high-throughput, a performance flow caching mode is available. In vMX release 15.1 there is one VFP image supplied, and the lite and performance modes are set within the Junos configuration on the VCP. In vMX release 14.1, Juniper provides two versions of VFP in the vMX package.

CAUTION If you are using the performance mode VFP, the CPU cores that are allocated to vMX interfaces will poll constantly (expect to see 100% usage) and for this reason you should use the *lite* version in your lab.

NOTE At the time of this writing, vMX supports one instance of the VCP although there is work in progress for vMX to support VCP redundancy. The current release of vMX assumes VCP and VFP are installed on the same physical server, although the architecture does allow for VCP and VFP to be installed on different physical servers.

MORE? There are three components to the software forwarding plane – a receive thread, a transmit thread, and a worker. The worker performs the lookups and tasks associated with packet processing and functionality that would normally be found in the Trio ASIC on the physical MX router. And the DPDK applies to the receive and transmit components. The receive thread moves packets from the NIC to the VFP and performs any pre-classification that may be required. The transmit thread moves packets from the worker to the physical NIC and includes a QoS scheduler to prioritize packets across six queues before being sent to the NIC.

vMX Virtual Machine Connectivity

Clearly the VFP VM and the VCP VM need to be able to communicate directly, so an internal bridge to enable this communication is required for each vMX instance.

An external bridge is also required. This is used to enable the management interface on the physical host to be used as the virtual management interface for both VCP and VFP. You will need to configure unique IP and MAC addresses for both the VCP and VFP.

This connectivity is shown in Figure 1.2.

On the VCP the internal em1 interface is placed within a routing-instance named `__juniper_private1__` however this routing-instance and em1 interface are not shown in the configuration. More on this in the troubleshooting section at the end of this book.

As the Linux KVM release of vMX is managed by an orchestration script, when vMX starts up this script will automatically create the two Linux bridges. On VMware, vSwitches must be created to achieve the same result.

MORE? For a deep dive on the architecture of vMX, see the forthcoming book, *The MX Series, 2nd Edition,* July 2016, from O'Reilly Media: http://shop.oreilly.com/product/0636920042709.do.

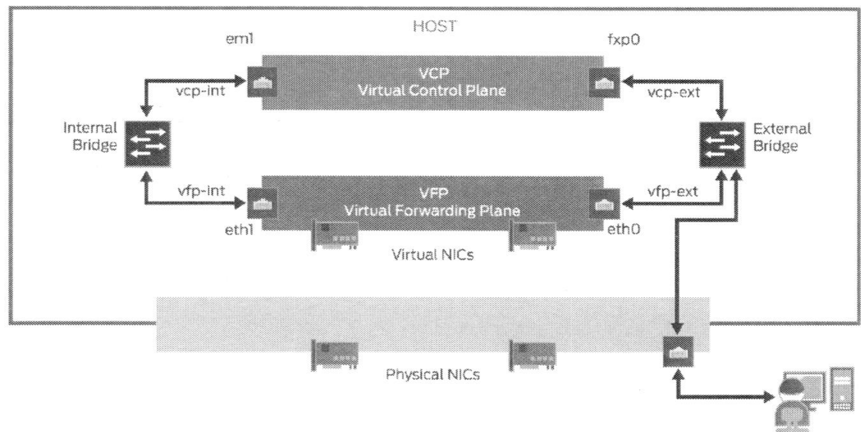

Figure 1.2 vMX Virtual Machine Communication

Data Interfaces and Performance

The vMX router supports the following types of interfaces:

- Gigabit Ethernet (ge)
- 10-Gigabit Ethernet (xe)
- 100-Gigabit Ethernet (et)

For data interfaces, there are a couple of techniques available for packet I/O depending on the required vMX throughput. Both of these techniques are designed to address inefficiencies when fully emulating the physical host.

Which one you choose ultimately depends on your use case for the vMX. Let's get through the specs first and then you can choose your lab setup.

Paravirtualization

For lab use and for throughputs of up to 3Gbps you can use paravirtualization using KVM's virtio drivers or on VMware ESXi by configuring vmxnet3. This paravirtualization technique is used to reduce overhead – essentially the network driver running in the guest virtual machine is aware of the virtual environment and interacts with the hypervisor to execute many functions.

PCI Passthrough with SR-IOV

For high performance use cases, at throughputs of 3Gbps or greater, PCI passthrough with single root I/O virtualization (SR-IOV) is required. Essentially SR-IOV is enabling the NIC to be connected directly to vMX. As data bypasses the hypervisor there is an increase in I/O performance because drivers in the VM are directly accessing the PCI device.

NOTE At the time of this writing, SR-IOV is fully supported on vMX 14.1 and 15.1 on KVM but not supported with vMX 15.1F4 running on VMware ESXi.

Sizing Information

Minimum Hardware and Software Requirements

Just for fun, all the labs in this Day One have been set up on a 2014 MacBook Pro (i7, 16GB RAM) running the Ubuntu VM as a nested virtual machine to give you an idea of the hardware specifications you'll need to complete the build discussed in this chapter. Please don't try this in production!

Please see the current release notes for the vMX release that you intend to deploy. On release 15.1F4 you are going to need at least 12GB RAM (2GB for VCP, 8GB for VFP, and 2GB for the Ubuntu host OS) and four vCPUs (one for VCP and three for VFP).

NOTE For more information on vMX running Junos 14.1 and 15.1 please refer to the release notes: http://www.juniper.net/techpubs/en_US/vmx14.1/information-products/topic-collections/release-notes/jd0e46.html, and, http://www.juniper.net/techpubs/en_US/vmx15.1/information-products/topic-collections/release-notes/jd0e46.html.

Licensing

Licensing is based on a combination of throughput and features, and the lowest available throughput license is 100Mbps. You don't need to be shifting multi-igabits of traffic to start with vMX. You can start small and pay-as-you-grow with vMX.

Below 1Gbps there are three throughput options: 100Mbps, 250Mbps and 500Mbps. These three license options include the full set of vMX *Premium Package* features but are limited to a RIB/FIB of 128,000 and 50 VPN instances (either Layer 2 or Layer 3 VPN).

At 1Gbps and above, licenses are a combination of features (Base, Advance, and Premium) and full duplex throughput (1G, 5G, 10G, 40G).

- Base – IP routing with 32,000 routes in the RIB/FIB.
  This license also provides basic Layer 2 functionality, Layer 2 bridging, and switching.
- Advance – All the features in the Base license, plus IP routing with routes up to 4 million in the RIB/FIB (8 million for 10G or above). Also enabled are IP and MPLS switching for unicast and multicast applications. Layer 2 features include Layer 2 VPN, VPLS, EVPN, VXLAN, and Layer 2 Circuit.
- Premium – All the features in the Base and Advance application packages. Layer 3 VPN for IP and multicast. Limited to 250 VPN instances (L2 and L3 VPN).
- Starting with Junos 15.1 vMX will allow for allow additive licenses. So you can start at, say, 500Mbps and add further capacity as needed later. Licenses are available on a perpetual or subscription basis.

NOTE The Base and Advance packages also include Layer 3 VPNs but are limited to a maximum of sixteen instances.

You can configure the physical MX Series routers to run in different network services modes.

A network services mode defines how the chassis recognizes and uses certain modules. When you set a physical MX router to `enhanced-ip` network services mode, only MPC/MIC modules and MS-DPC modules are powered on in the chassis. This also means that the network services mode can restrict the available Layer 2, Layer 2.5, and Layer 3 features that are available on the MX chassis. For example, if you configure enhanced-ethernet mode then certain BGP functions will be restricted and there will be no support for Layer 3 VPNs, which also means that unless you are using the Enhanced IP mode there is will be limited support for Layer 3 features, although Layer 2.5 features such as VPLS will still be supported.

You are probably asking yourself, why is all this important for the vMX ?

NOTE An unlicensed vMX instance is locked to a network-services mode of enhanced-ethernet and this means that only the Layer 2.5 features are available. BGP is available but data plane support applies only to Ethernet and MPLS.

As soon as you apply a license to vMX (which includes a trial license) the network services mode is automatically changed to `enhanced-ip` and all the Layer 2 and Layer 3 features become available up to the limits of the applied license.

You can find out more about the Enhanced Ethernet mode restrictions at http://www.juniper.net/techpubs/en_US/junos15.1/topics/concept/chassis-mx-series-junos-features-restrictions.html.

Chapter 2

Getting Started with vMX on KVM

Okay, now that you have some background on vMX the fun can begin! This chapter walks you through a complete build of vMX, starting with the installation and set up of the Ubuntu host OS for vMX.

Once the host OS is ready, with the prerequisite packages installed, you will be able to see how vMX is built and configured – from orchestration scripts to configuration files.

Installing vMX

At the time of this writing, the version of vMX available for trial is running Junos OS 15.1F4, so that is the version used here. You can download the most recent, up-to-date trial at http://www.juniper.net/us/en/dm/free-vmx-trial/.

Be sure to check for new releases depending on when you are reading these pages.

Juniper recommends the use of Ubuntu 14.04.1 LTS for vMX host operating system and the KVM hypervisor, although 14.04.1 is not the latest release of Ubuntu 14.04, so bear this in mind when downloading the software. The installation of vMX on Ubuntu is a straightforward process.

NOTE If you are doing this lab build on a MacBook or PC with Ubuntu running as a VM, allocate at least 50GB Hard Drive, 12GB RAM, four vCPUs, and two vNICs (one for management, one for data) to the Ubuntu VM. Also the VM must be enabled to support Nested Virtualization within the VM.

Ubuntu Host OS Installation

First enable Intel VT-d in the host machine's BIOS. Once this is done, it's time to install Ubuntu.

Download a copy of Ubuntu 14.04.1 server from http://old-releases.ubuntu.com/releases/14.04.1/

If you wish, you can try the most recent version of 14.04 at http://www.ubuntu.com/download/server but bear in mind that 14.04.1 is the release that Juniper recommends.

Create a bootable USB drive. Ubuntu provides instructions showing how to do this on Windows (http://www.ubuntu.com/download/desktop/create-a-usb-stick-on-windows) and on OS X (http://www.ubuntu.com/download/desktop/create-a-usb-stick-on-mac-osx).

Boot the installer using the Ubuntu 14.04 boot image you just created, selecting *Install Ubuntu Server* as shown in Figure 2.1.

Figure 2.1 Installing Ubuntu

Go through the steps for installation, selecting the correct language and keyboard. Use DHCP or manual IP addressing, as appropriate. You will also need to set a hostname and configure a local user account. To keep things simple, use the "Guided – use entire disk" partition layout with LVM, if you prefer.

When you are provided with a "Software selection" screen be sure to select only OpenSSH Server and Virtual Machine host as shown in Figure 2.2.

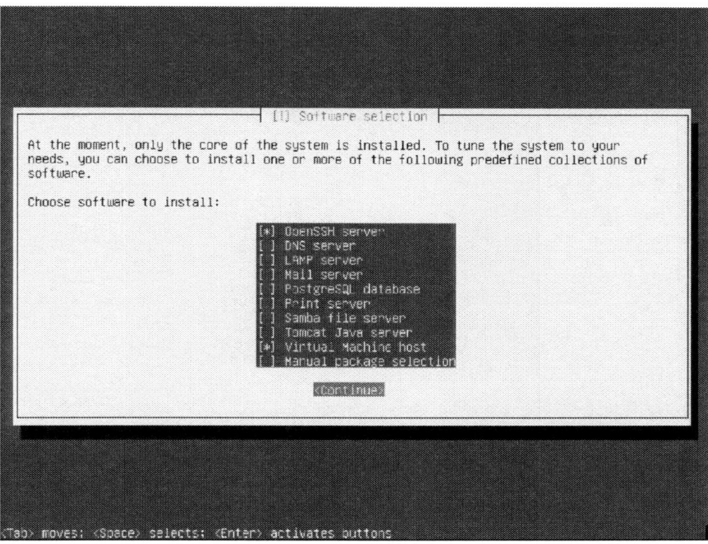

Figure 2.2 Ubuntu Package Selection

Install the GRUB boot loader when asked, and then after a few moments the installation will finish and the installation will reboot the server.

Now, log in to the server to set up management NIC networking. This is done by editing the file */etc/network/interfaces*. To use DHCP, set the management Ethernet interface setting as:

```
auto eth0
iface eth0 inet dhcp
```

For static addressing, configure it similar to the following, using your preferred IP schema:

```
auto eth0
iface eth0 inet static
        address 192.168.100.200
        netmask 255.255.255.0
        network 192.168.100.0
        broadcast 192.168.100.255
        gateway 192.168.100.254
        dns-nameservers 192.168.100.254
        dns-search dinham.local
```

Configure the second NIC (the data NIC for vMX) to come up on boot, but with no IP addressing:

```
auto eth1
iface eth1 inet manual
```

Save the file and quit to the shell, and restart networking to load in the new configuration:

```
sudo ifdown eth0 ; sudo ifup eth0
```

Now you will be able to SSH in to the host. As mentioned, 14.04.1 is the qualified release and updating all of the installed packages may cause issues. Updating the packages is not a necessary step for vMX, but if you wish to update the packages anyway, on Ubuntu it is done using the APT package manager:

```
mdinham@vmx-day1:~$ sudo apt-get upgrade
[sudo] password for mdinham:
Reading package lists... Done
Building dependency tree
Reading state information... Done
Calculating upgrade... Done
The following packages have been kept back:
  linux-generic-lts-utopic linux-headers-generic-lts-utopic
  linux-image-generic-lts-utopic
The following packages will be upgraded:
<snip>
156 to upgrade, 0 to newly install, 0 to remove and 3 not to upgrade.
Need to get 70.8 MB of archives.
After this operation, 19.8 MB of additional disk space will be used.
Do you want to continue? [Y/n] y
```

Key in "y" to continue (Yes) and after a short time your vMX host OS will be updated and ready to use.

Preparing the System for vMX

It's now time to install the prerequisite packages for vMX.

Upgrading the Kernel

Depending on the exact version of Ubuntu 14.04 server that was installed, you may also need to upgrade the kernel packages. Juniper recommends that you use Linux Kernel 3.13.0-32 generic. You can skip this step if you are using 14.04.1:

```
mdinham@vmx-day1:~$ sudo apt-get install linux-firmware linux-image-3.13.0.32-
generic linux-image-extra-3.13.0.32-generic linux-headers-3.13.0.32-generic
mdinham@vmx-day1:/etc/grub.d$ sudo update-grub
```

Install system prerequisite packages

Some of these packages will already have been installed during the Ubuntu install process, but the complete list is provided below. Again this is done using `apt-get`:

```
mdinham@vmx-day1:~$ sudo apt-get install bridge-utils qemu-kvm libvirt-bin python python-
netifaces vnc4server libyaml-dev python-yaml numactl libparted0-dev libpciaccess-
dev libnuma-dev libyajl-dev libxml2-dev libglib2.0-dev libnl-dev python-pip python-
dev libxml2-dev libxslt-dev
```

The prerequisites and any package dependencies will now be installed.

Upgrading to Libvirt 1.2.19

Libvirt is open source software for managing VMs. There is an API library, a daemon (libvirtd), and a command line utility (virsh). Juniper uses libvirt to create and manage vMX instances.

Ubuntu 14.04 ships with version 1.2.2 of libvirt. This version works fine for the lite mode of the PFE but as the performance mode requires an upgrade to 1.2.19, it's handy that you know how to do the upgrade.

NOTE I recommend that you skip this libvirt upgrade if you are building vMX for lab purposes, or if you plan to run the virtual forwarding plane in Lite mode.

First check the installed version of libvirt:

```
mdinham@vmx-day1:~$ libvirtd --version
libvirtd (libvirt) 1.2.2
mdinham@vmx-day1:~$ virsh version
Compiled against library: libvirt 1.2.2
Using library: libvirt 1.2.2
Using API: QEMU 1.2.2
Running hypervisor: QEMU 2.0.0
```

To upgrade to libvirt 1.2.19, perform the following steps:

1. Download the source code. You can easily do this using the `wget` command line tool:

```
mdinham@vmx-day1:~$ cd /tmp
mdinham@vmx-day1:/tmp$ wget http://libvirt.org/sources/libvirt-1.2.19.tar.gz
```

2. Now, uncompress the tar file and perform the following steps to configure and build libvirt. Before building and installing the upgraded version, the existing libvirtd service must be stopped:

```
mdinham@vmx-day1:/tmp$ tar -xzf libvirt-1.2.19.tar.gz
mdinham@vmx-day1:/tmp$ sudo service libvirt-bin stop
```

3. You can now configure, build, and install the new version of libvirt:

```
mdinham@vmx-day1:~$ cd libvirt-1.2.19/
mdinham@vmx-day1:/tmp/libvirt-1.2.19$ ./configure --prefix=/usr --localstatedir=/ --with-
numactl
mdinham@vmx-day1:/tmp/libvirt-1.2.19$ make
mdinham@vmx-day1:/tmp/libvirt-1.2.19$ sudo make install
mdinham@vmx-day1:/tmp/libvirt-1.2.19$ sudo ldconfig
```

At this point the new versions of libvirt and the command line tools are installed. The installer will have overwritten the Ubuntu libvirt configuration file. If you want to be able to use libvirt as a user other than root, then you will need to make a couple of tweaks to the libvirtd configuration file. The connection is made to libvirt using UNIX sockets, so you simply need to modify the configuration file to specify the group containing the non-root users to be allowed, and change the permissions. Open up `/etc/libvirt/libvirtd.conf` and modify the following options as below (note the '*d*' on the end of libvirt – Ubuntu creates a group called *libvirtd* not *libvirt*):

```
unix_sock_group = "libvirtd"
unix_sock_ro_perms = "0777"
unix_sock_rw_perms = "0770"
auth_unix_ro = "none"
auth_unix_rw = "none"
```

You will also need to edit */etc/group* and add your user name to the libvirtd group:

```
libvirtd:x:111:mdinham
```

4. You can now verify that things have been installed correctly. Start the libvirt process if everything is okay, it will run as a daemon and not die immediately on startup:

```
mdinham@vmx-day1:/tmp/libvirt-1.2.19$ sudo service libvirt-bin start
libvirt-bin start/running, process 41916
mdinham@vmx-day1:/tmp/libvirt-1.2.19$ ps auxw | grep libvirtd
root      41916  0.2  0.1 257804 11156 ?       Sl   17:33   0:00 /usr/sbin/libvirtd -d
mdinham   42016  0.0  0.0  11752  2156 pts/0    S+   17:33   0:00 grep --color=auto libvirtd
```

5. Excellent. This looks good. Let's check again on the versions of the binaries:

```
mdinham@vmx-day1~$ libvirtd --version
libvirtd (libvirt) 1.2.19
mdinham@vmx-day1:~$ virsh --version
1.2.19
mdinham@vmx-day1:~$ virsh --connect qemu:///system version
Compiled against library: libvirt 1.2.19
Using library: libvirt 1.2.19
Using API: QEMU 1.2.19
Running hypervisor: QEMU 2.0.0
```

All looks good - now the Ubuntu host is ready for vMX and you can move on with the installation and configuration of the vMX itself.

Installing and Configuring vMX

For this lab-based build, you should use virtio for the virtual NIC. As mentioned earlier, there are two modes of VFP operation – a *lite* mode PFE for labs, and a *performance* mode for normal operation. You should use the lite mode, which is the default configuration. Let's get going!

Download vMX from http://www.juniper.net/us/en/dm/free-vmx-trial/ and extract the package in your home directory:

```
mdinham@vmx-day1:~$ ls
vmx-15.1F4.15.tgz
mdinham@vmx-day1:~$ tar -xzf vmx-15.1F4.15.tgz
mdinham@vmx-day1:~$ cd vmx-15.1F4-3/
```

Let's have a look at the vMX package contents:

```
mdinham@vmx-day1:~/vmx-15.1F4-3$ ls
config  docs  drivers  env  images  scripts  vmx.sh
```

The vMX images are located within the "images" directory. You should use the VCP image (jinstall64-vmx-15.1F4.15-domestic.img) and the VFP image (vFPC-20151203.img). Also provided is vmxhdd.img, the software image for VCP file storage:

```
mdinham@vmx-day1:~/vmx-15.1F4-3$ ls images/
jinstall64-vmx-15.1F4.15-domestic.img  jinstall64-vmx-15.1F4.15-domestic.tgz  metadata_
usb.img  vFPC-20151203.img  vmxhdd.img
```

NOTE If you are using vMX 14.1 there are two software image files for the FPC. Use the "-lite" image.

The configuration files are located within the "config" directory. The main config for vMX is defined in vmx.conf, and the configuration for vMX interfaces (virtio) within vmx-junosdev.conf:

```
mdinham@vmx-day1:~/vmx-15.1F4-3$ ls config/
samples  vmx.conf  vmx-junosdev.conf
```

Configuring and Deploying a Single Instance of vMX on KVM

To begin, you need to set up the vMX configuration file. By default, this is done by editing config/vmx.conf, however, you can create your own configuration file and and use the script --cfg option to specify it. The configuration file uses YAML format.

NOTE Multiple instances of vMX can run on the same physical host, you simply need to define additional configuration files.

Host Configuration

Edit the vMX configuration file:

```
mdinham@vmx-day1:~/vmx-15.1F4-3/config$ sudo vi vmx.conf
```

First set an instance identifier for the vMX instance, here it is set to `vmx1`.

Now update the configuration file to reflect the absolute path to the img files.

Set the "host-management-interface" to be management interface on the physical host. This interface will be bridged to the vMX instance own management interfaces on the VCP and VFP:

```
#Configuration on the host side - management interface, VM images etc.
HOST:
    identifier                : vmx1   # Maximum 4 characters
    host-management-interface : eth0
    routing-engine-image      : "/home/mdinham/vmx-15.1F4-3/images/jinstall64-vmx-15.1F4.15-
domestic.img"
    routing-engine-hdd        : "/home/mdinham/vmx-15.1F4-3/images/vmxhdd.img"
    forwarding-engine-image   : "/home/mdinham/vmx-15.1F4-3/images/vFPC-20151203.img"
```

VCP and VFP Configuration

Now let's configure the parameters for the control and forwarding planes. These are also defined in the vmx.conf configuration file.

For vMX 15.1, allocate one vCPU and 2GB RAM to VCP, and three vCPUs and 8GB RAM to VFP. Or for vMX 14.1 you should allocate 1GB to the control plane and 6GB to the forwarding plane.

NOTE If you are tight on resources in your lab I completed the labs in this book running Ubuntu as a nested VM on my MacBook. I allocated 4GB to the forwarding plane (which is below the Juniper recommendation of 8GB for 15.1) and the forwarding plane loaded. 4GB could be fine for your lab purposes depending on the features and version of vMX that you are using. 1GB should be the absolute minimum on the control plane. Please don't do this in a production environment because it is not a Juniper supported configuration and if something goes wrong, JTAC won't help you!

Note below that the VFP device type is set to `virtio` for the interfaces.

You will see here that a bridge is also defined – this is the management interface bridge mentioned earlier. For the control plane and forwarding plane, you need to also set an IP address – make sure to use an IP on the same subnet as the host management network:

```
---
#External bridge configuration
BRIDGES:
    - type  : external
      name  : br-ext              # Max 10 characters

---
#vRE VM parameters
CONTROL_PLANE:
    vcpus        : 1
    memory-mb    : 2048
    console_port: 8601

    interfaces  :
      - type      : static
```

```
        ipaddr     : 192.168.100.201
        macaddr    : "0A:00:DD:C0:DE:0E"

---
#vPFE VM parameters
FORWARDING_PLANE:
    memory-mb    : 8192
    vcpus        : 3
    console_port: 8602
    device-type : virtio

    interfaces  :
      - type       : static
        ipaddr     : 192.168.100.202
        macaddr    : "0A:00:DD:C0:DE:10"
```

The default MAC addresses used in the configuration file are taken from the locally administered MAC address ranges. For the time being, you are just getting a single instance of vMX running, so no other VCP or VFP parameters need to be changed at this point.

Interface Configuration (virtio)

Now let's configure the interface for the vMX. You will only be using one interface in this lab setup, but many more can be configured. Just comment out the other interfaces, leaving only ge-0/0/0 defined:

```
---
#Interfaces
JUNOS_DEVICES:
 - interface : ge-0/0/0
 mac-address : "02:06:0A:0E:FF:F0"
 description : "ge-0/0/0 interface"
```

NOTE For an SR-IOV configuration, things are done slightly differently as there are few additional parameters to configure. SR-IOV is out of scope for this lab but not too terribly difficult. Try it yourself if needed – there are sample configuration files for both virtio and SR-IOV in the vMX package directory `config/samples`.

You also need to create Linux bridges to link vMX ge-0/0/0 to an interface on the physical host. By default, this is done in the device binding configuration file, `config/vmx-junosdev.conf`, however, you can create your own configuration file and use the --cfg option to specify it. The vMX orchestration scripts do all the heavy lifting for you to set up the bridges.

The device binding file uses YAML, enabling a flexible configuration for connecting VFP endpoints to a physical NIC, another vMX instance, or to another Linux bridge.

The parameters in the configuration are:

- link-name: This is the name of the Linux bridge, it can be up to 15 characters long and must be unique.
- mtu: The default is 1500 but can be increased to 9500.
- endpoint: This can be a vMX instance (`junos_dev`), a host interface (`host_dev`), or a bridge (`bridge_dev`). For endpoint type `junos_dev` the setting `vm_name` respresents the actual name of the vMX instance. `dev_name` represents the interface name or bridge name.

You need to create a new Linux bridge between host interface eth1 and ge-0/0/0 on vmx1. Modify the configuration file `config/vmx-junosdev.conf` like this:

```
##############################################################
#
#  vmx-junos-dev.conf
#  - Config file for junos device bindings.
#  - Uses YAML syntax.
#  - Leave a space after ":" to specify the parameter value.
#  - For physical NIC, set the 'type' as 'host_dev'
#  - For junos devices, set the 'type' as 'junos_dev' and
#    set the mandatory parameter 'vm-name' to the name of
#    the vPFE where the device exists
#  - For bridge devices, set the 'type' as 'bridge_dev'
#
##############################################################
interfaces :

     - link_name  : vmx_link
       mtu        : 1500
       endpoint_1 :
         - type        : junos_dev
           vm_name     : vmx1
           dev_name    : ge-0/0/0
       endpoint_2 :
         - type        : host_dev
           dev_name    : eth1
```

You can see that the lab has defined a single Linux bridge named `vmx_link` and it will use this bridge to link ge-0/0/0 on the instance vmx1 to the host physical interface eth1. You will need to use the vMX orchestration script to activate this binding and create the Linux bridge, but let's do that once you have successfully deployed the vMX instance.

Deploying Your Instance of vMX

Now that the vMX has been configured, it's time for you to deploy your instance. This is done using the orchestration script. Your vMX instance will be created and automatically started by the script.

Make sure that you specify the `-lv` parameter for verbose logging because this is really going to help you out with troubleshooting if the scripts run into a problem:

```
mdinham@vmx-day1:~/vmx-15.1F4-3$ sudo ./vmx.sh -lv --install
==================================================
   Welcome to VMX
==================================================
Date..........................................02/23/16 12:59:00
VMX Identifier................................vmx1
Config file...................................../home/mdinham/vmx-15.1F4-3/config/vmx.
conf
Build Directory................................./home/mdinham/vmx-15.1F4-3/build/vmx1
Environment file................................/home/mdinham/vmx-15.1F4-3/env/ubuntu_
virtio.env
Junos Device Type...............................virtio
Initialize scripts .............................{OK]
Copy images to build directory..................[OK]
==================================================
    VMX Environment Setup Completed
==================================================
==================================================
    VMX Install & Start
==================================================
Linux distribution..............................ubuntu
Check GRUB......................................[Disabled]
Installation status of qemu-kvm.................[OK]
Installation status of libvirt-bin..............[OK]
Installation status of bridge-utils.............[OK]
Installation status of python...................[OK]
Installation status of libyaml-dev..............[OK]
Installation status of python-yaml..............[OK]
Installation status of numactl..................[OK]
Installation status of libnuma-dev..............[OK]
Installation status of libparted0-dev...........[OK]
Installation status of libpciaccess-dev.........[OK]
Installation status of libyajl-dev..............[OK]
Installation status of libxml2-dev..............[OK]
Installation status of libglib2.0-dev...........[OK]
Installation status of libnl-dev................[OK]
Check Kernel Version............................[Disabled]
Check Qemu Version..............................[Disabled]
Check libvirt Version...........................[Disabled]
Check virsh connectivity........................[OK]
IXGBE Enabled...................................[Disabled]
==================================================
    Pre-Install Checks Completed
==================================================
Check for VM vcp-vmx1...........................[Not Running]
Check for VM vfp-vmx1...........................[Not Running]
Cleanup VM states...............................[OK]
Check if bridge br-ext exists...................[No]
Cleanup VM bridge br-ext........................[OK]
Cleanup VM bridge br-int-vmx1...................[OK]
==================================================
    VMX Stop Completed
==================================================
Check VCP image.................................[OK]
Check VFP image.................................[OK]
VMX Model.......................................FPC
Check VCP Config image..........................[OK]
```

```
Check management interface........................[OK]
Setup huge pages to 8192..........................[OK]
Attempt to kill libvirt...........................[OK]
Attempt to start libvirt..........................[OK]
Sleep 2 secs......................................[OK]
Check libvirt support for hugepages...............[OK]
==================================================
    System Setup Completed
==================================================
Get Management Address of eth0....................[OK]
Generate libvirt files............................[OK]
Sleep 2 secs......................................[OK]
Find configured management interface..............eth0
Find existing management gateway..................eth0
Check if eth0 is already enslaved to br-ext.......[No]
Gateway interface needs change....................[Yes]
Create br-ext.....................................[OK]
Get Management Gateway............................192.168.100.254
Flush eth0........................................[OK]
Start br-ext......................................[OK]
Bind eth0 to br-ext...............................[OK]
Get Management MAC................................00:0c:29:51:0c:44
Assign Management MAC 00:0c:29:51:0c:44...........[OK]
Add default gw 192.168.100.254....................[OK]
Create br-int-vmx1................................[OK]
Start br-int-vmx1.................................[OK]
Check and start default bridge....................[OK]
Define vcp-vmx1...................................[OK]
Define vfp-vmx1...................................[OK]
Wait 2 secs.......................................[OK]
Start vcp-vmx1....................................[OK]
Start vfp-vmx1....................................[Failed]
error: Failed to start domain vfp-vmx1
error: internal error: early end of file from monitor: possible problem:
file_ram_alloc: can't mmap RAM pages: Cannot allocate memory
Log file..........................................
    /home/mdinham/vmx-15.1F4-3/build/vmx1/logs/vmx_1456232340.log
==================================================
 Aborted!. 1 error(s) and 0 warning(s)
==================================================
```

If anything goes wrong the installer will abort and you will be given an error message, just as is shown here where the VFP isn't starting because the Ubuntu host does not have enough memory assigned. Because this is the lab and I'm running the Ubuntu KVM server itself as a VM, it's a quick fix to assign some more memory to it.

Once corrected, the installer completes and starts up the vMX – remember there are two VMs that must be started, the VCP and the VFP:

```
Start vcp-vmx1....................................[OK]
Start vfp-vmx1....................................[OK]
Wait 2 secs.......................................[OK]
==================================================
    VMX Bringup Completed
==================================================
```

```
Check if br-ext is created........................[Created]
Check if br-int-vmx1 is created...................[Created]
Check if VM vcp-vmx1 is running...................[Running]
Check if VM vfp-vmx1 is running...................[Running]
Check if tap interface vcp_ext-vmx1 exists........[OK]
Check if tap interface vcp_int-vmx1 exists........[OK]
Check if tap interface vfp_ext-vmx1 exists........[OK]
Check if tap interface vfp_int-vmx1 exists........[OK]
==================================================
    VMX Status Verification Completed.
==================================================
Log file..........................................
    /home/mdinham/vmx-15.1F4-3/build/vmx1/logs/vmx_1456232854.log
==================================================
    Thankyou for using VMX
==================================================
```

Now let's take a quick look at what the orchestration script has done to deploy this vMX instance. All the images and settings for a particular vMX instance are located within the `build/` directory. Here you can see that for the instance vMX1 there are three directories – `images`, `logs`, and `xml`:

```
mdinham@vmx-day1:~/vmx-15.1F4-3$ ls build/vmx1
images  logs  xml
```

The `images` subdirectory is where the software image files are located for the vMX instance. When you deploy a vMX instance, the orchestration script will copy the package image files to this vMX instance-specific location:

```
mdinham@vmx-day1:~/vmx-15.1F4-3/build/vmx1$ ls images
jinstall64-vmx-15.1F4.15-domestic.img  vFPC-20151203.img  vmxhdd.img
```

This also enables you to have multiple vMX on the same system, each running different versions of the Junos OS. The image file `vmxhdd.img` is used by the VCP to store configuration information.

The `logs` directory is where the orchestration scripts place the log files. This is a good place to look if you have any problems managing your vMX deployment or during a stop/start operation.

The `xml` directory is where copies of the libvirt XML files are stored. These XML files contain the configuration data for the Internal/External bridges and the VCP/VFP virtual machines. Later in this chapter there is more on how librvirt uses these configuration files to start up the vMX.

You might also be interested in knowing how much disk space an instance of vMX will require. It's around 2.1G – this is because all of the image files are copied to the vMX instance specific build area:

```
mdinham@vmx-day1:~/vmx-15.1F4-3/build$ du -sh vmx1
2.1G      vmx1
```

Linux Bridges and Managing a Virtio Binding

At this point the vMX is running and since you already configured the binding when you edited the `config/vmx-junosdev.conf` file, all that remains to be done is to activate the configuration. But first let's review what Linux bridges the vMX script just created when the vMX instance was deployed. This is done using the shell `brctl show` command:

```
mdinham@vmx-day1:~/mx-15.1F4-3$  brctl show

bridge name     bridge id               STP enabled     interfaces
br-ext          8000.000c29510c44       yes             br-ext-nic
                                                        eth0
                                                        vcp_ext-vmx1
                                                        vfp_ext-vmx1
br-int-vmx1     8000.5254008f5d25       yes             br-int-vmx1-nic
                                                        vcp_int-vmx1
                                                        vfp_int-vmx1
```

You can see the bridges that the vMX automatically creates when started, and as shown in the output above are:

Bridge "br-ext" is the external bridge that is used for management of the vMX and the KVM host. You can see here that eth0 on the physical host and the management interfaces on the VCP and VFP have been added to this bridge. This bridge can be shared by multiple vMX instances.

Bridge "br-int-vmx1" is the internal bridge that is used for communication between the VCP and VFP, that together make a particular vMX instance. You can see here that the internal interfaces on the VCP and VFP have been added to this bridge. Separate internal bridges are required per vMX instance, which is why this one is named with the "-vmx1" suffix.

Now it's time to activate the virtio binding. First you can check that it has not already been activated. Again you will be using the orchestration script that Juniper provide with vMX:

```
mdinham@vmx-day1:~/vmx-15.1F4-3$ sudo ./vmx.sh --bind-check
Checking package ethtool.........................[OK]
Check Link vmx_link(ge-0.0.0-vmx1, eth1).........[Not Present]
```

Well, from the output it is pretty clear that the binding is missing. This time using the `bind-dev` option will create the binding:

```
mdinham@vmx-day1:~/vmx-15.1F4-3$ sudo ./vmx.sh --bind-dev
Checking package ethtool.........................[OK]
Bind Link vmx_link(ge-0.0.0-vmx1, eth1)..........[OK]
Numa node for eth1...............................-1
Cores servicing numa node -1.....................
Pid of vfp-vmx1..................................20804
Pin vhost-20804 (PID=20807) to cores ............taskset: failed to parse CPU list:
```

```
[Failed]
Pin vhost-20804 (PID=20806) to cores ............taskset: failed to parse CPU list:
[Failed]
Pin vhost-20804 (PID=20805) to cores ............taskset: failed to parse CPU list:
[Failed]
```

The taskset command is used to achieve better performance in virtio mode, however, the error can be ignored for the purposes of your lab so long as the bindings are present:

```
mdinham@vmx-day1:~/vmx-15.1F4-3$ ./vmx.sh --bind-check
Checking package ethtool.........................[OK]
Check Link vmx_link(ge-0.0.0-vmx1, eth1).........[OK]
```

Let's take another look at the Linux bridges. This time there should be a newly created bridge.

In the configuration file it was specified that the bridge should be called `vmx_link` and that it links together eth1 on the physical host with ge-0/0/0 on the vMX. You can see here that the bridge has been created exactly as configured:

```
mdinham@vmx-day1:~/vmx-15.1F4-3$ brctl show
bridge name     bridge id               STP enabled     interfaces
br-ext          8000.000c29510c44       yes             br-ext-nic
                                                        eth0
                                                        vcp_ext-vmx1
                                                        vfp_ext-vmx1
br-int-vmx1     8000.5254009ee238       yes             br-int-vmx1-nic
                                                        vcp_int-vmx1
                                                        vfp_int-vmx1
vmx_link        8000.000c29510c4e       no              eth1
                                                        ge-0.0.0-vmx1
```

Try It Yourself: Connect vMX to a KVM Host Interface and Monitor Traffic With tcpdump

Bind a host interface with the configuration as demonstrated in this chapter and test to see if you can send traffic from the vMX via the physical interface. Use tcpdump on the KVM host interface to monitor traffic being bridged between the vMX and the host interface.

Modify the configuration if you wish, and then apply and check the new binding again. This configuration will bind ge-0-0/0 to eth1 (adapt to your environment if necessary):

```
interfaces :
     - link_name  : vmx_link
       mtu        : 1500
       endpoint_1 :
         - type       : junos_dev
           vm_name    : vmx1
           dev_name   : ge-0/0/0
       endpoint_2 :
         - type       : host_dev
           dev_name   : eth1
```

Connect to the vMX Instances

You can now connect to the vMX via the serial console. This is done using the *vmx.sh* script again.

Serial Console

You will need to specify `vcp` (control plane) or `vfp` (forwarding plane), as well as the instance name as options. In the example below, a console connection is being made to the VCP on the instance named "vmx1":

```
mdinham@vmx-day1:~/vmx-15.1F4-3$ sudo ./vmx.sh --console vcp vmx1
--
Login Console Port For vcp-vmx1 - 8601
Press Ctrl-] to exit anytime
--
Trying ::1...
Trying 127.0.0.1...
Connected to localhost.
Escape character is '^]'.


Amnesiac (ttyd0)

login:
```

NOTE To break out of a console connection to the vMX use the standard "Ctrl-]" escape keyboard sequence. The default login credentials for the VCP are root, no password, and for the VFP root, root.

NOTE If you are new to the Junos CLI, see *Day One: Exploring the Junos CLI, Second Edition* at http://www.juniper.net/dayone.

SSH

Remember that the virtual management interface on the VCP (interface fxp0) is bridged to the physical host management interface and multiple instances of vMX are able to share this external bridge.

This means that you can also use SSH to access the Junos OS on the vMX. I'm sure you will find that using SSH to configure vMX makes things a lot easier for your lab build. It's done like this:

Console in to the vMX instance and set an IP address on the management interface. As the physical host's management interface is bridged to the VCP management interface, use an IP address from the same subnet as the physical host's management IP:

```
set interfaces fxp0 unit 0 family inet address 192.168.100.201/24
```

Then enable the SSH service:

```
set system services ssh
```

Also set the hostname, and a password for the root user, if you have not done so already:

```
set system host-name vmx1
set system root-authentication plain-text-password
```

Now commit the configuration and exit the console session. You should now be able to SSH directly to the vMX using the IP address that was just configured on the fxp0 interface:

```
mdinham@vmx-day1:~/vmx-15.1F4-3$ ssh root@192.168.100.201
Password:
Last login: Tue Feb 23 13:43:14 2016 from 192.168.100.200
--- JUNOS 15.1F4.15 built 2015-12-23 20:22:39 UTC
root@vmx1%
```

NOTE The VFP management interface will be assigned an IP address using DHCP and will be set to the IP address that you configured in the vmx.conf configuration file. As the VCP management interface fxp0 does not currently support DHCP, the IP address must be configured manually.

Managing Licenses

You have now installed Ubuntu and deployed an instance of vMX, but before you can do anything else you need to apply a license to the vMX. This is done via the virtual control plane on Junos.

If you have not already downloaded a trial license key then do so at http://www.juniper.net/us/en/dm/free-vmx-trial/ and select the key for a 60-day 50Mbps trial.

Adding a license to the vMX

1. Connect to the vMX, log in as *root*, and start the Junos CLI:

```
root@% cli
root>
```

2. Copy the license to the vMX and add the key file by specifying a file name, or do it directly by pasting the key in to the terminal as shown here:

```
root> request system license add ?
Possible completions:
  <filename>            Filename (URL, local, remote, or floppy)
  terminal              Use login terminal
root> request system license add terminal
[Type ^D at a new line to end input,
```

```
 enter blank line between each license key]
<KEY REMOVED - see http://www.juniper.net/us/en/dm/free-vmx-trial/>
add license complete (no errors)
```

3. To verify that the license has been installed correctly use the `show system license` command. `VMX-BANDWIDTH` indicates the licensed bandwidth and `VMX-SCALE` indicates the application package. (VMX-SCALE 1 is the Base package, VMX-SCALE 2 is the Advance package, and VMX-SCALE 3 is the Premium package):

```
root@vmx1> show system license
License usage:
                                 Licenses     Licenses    Licenses    Expiry
  Feature name                       used    installed      needed
  scale-subscriber                      0         1000           0    permanent
  scale-l2tp                            0         1000           0    permanent
  scale-mobile-ip                       0         1000           0    permanent
  VMX-BANDWIDTH                        50           50           0    60 days
  VMX-SCALE                             3            3           0    60 days

Licenses installed:
  License identifier: E421992502
  License version: 4
  Software Serial Number: 20151020
  Customer ID: vMX-JuniperEval
  Features:
    vmx-bandwidth-50m - vmx-bandwidth-50m
      count-down, Original validity: 60 days
    vmx-feature-premium - vmx-feature-premium
      count-down, Original validity: 60 days
```

Here you can see that the trial license has been applied as expected: 50Mbps Premium Features, on a 60-day countdown. After 60 days, the throughput will drop down to 0Mbps.

You can also check the licensing for the PFE:

```
root> show pfe statistics traffic bandwidth
    Configured Bandwidth         : 50000000 bps
    Bandwidth                    : 0 bps
    Average Bandwidth            : 0 bps
```

The vMX is now ready for your lab!

Managing vMX

Let's run the vMX orchestration script without any options just to see what it can do:

```
mdinham@vmx-day1:~/vmx-15.1F4-3$ ./vmx.sh

Usage: vmx.sh [CONTROL OPTIONS]
       vmx.sh [LOGGING OPTIONS] [CONTROL OPTIONS]
       vmx.sh [JUNOS-DEV BIND OPTIONS]
       vmx.sh [CONSOLE LOGIN OPTIONS]
```

```
    CONTROL OPTIONS:
       --install                   : Install And Start vMX
       --start                     : Start vMX
       --stop                      : Stop vMX
       --restart                   : Restart vMX
       --status                    : Check Status Of vMX
       --cleanup                   : Stop vMX And Cleanup Build Files
       --cfg <file>                : Override With The Specified vmx.conf File
       --env <file>                : Override With The Specified Environment .env File
       --build <directory>         : Override With The Specified Directory for Temporary
Files
       --help                      : This Menu

    LOGGING OPTIONS:
       -l                          : Enable Logging
       -lv                         : Enable Verbose Logging
       -lvf                        : Enable Foreground Verbose Logging

    JUNOS-DEV BIND OPTIONS:
       --bind-dev                  : Bind Junos Devices
       --unbind-dev                : Unbind Junos Devices
       --bind-check                : Check Junos Device Bindings
       --cfg <file>                : Override With The Specified vmx-junosdev.conf File

    CONSOLE LOGIN OPTIONS:
       --console [vcp|vfp] [vmx_id]   : Login to the Console of VCP/VFP

    VFP Image OPTIONS:
       --vfp-info <VFP Image Path>    : Display Information About The Specified vFP image

Copyright(c) Juniper Networks,
```

Use these options with the *vmx.sh* script to stop, start, restart, verify, and clean up an existing vMX:

- `cfg file`: Use the specified configuration file. The default file is config/vmx.conf. If you do not specify a startup configuration file with this option, the default file is used.
- `cleanup`: Stop the vMX and clean up the vMX instance. This option will also remove any Linux bridges.

CAUTION Be careful with this `cleanup` option because it will delete all of the Junos configuration for a vMX instance!

- `restart`: Stop and start a running vMX.
- `start`: Start the vMX instance.
- `status`: Verify the status of a deployed vMX.
- `stop`: Stop vMX without cleaning up build files so that the vMX can be started quickly without setup performed by the `--install` option.

Libvirt

You might be interested in what the *vmx.sh* script does with libvirt and virsh behind the scenes. Let's take a look where libvirt stores the configuration files for the vMX virtual machines:

```
mdinham@vmx-day1:~/vmx-15.1F4-3$ cd /etc/libvirt/qemu/
mdinham@vmx-day1:/etc/libvirt/qemu$ ls
networks  vcp-vmx1.xml  vfp-vmx1.xml
```

The `networks` directory is where the Linux bridge configurations are created by virsh, and the two xml files `vcp-vmx1.xml` and `vfp-vmx1.xml`, are the actual configuration files for the vMX VMs. If you take a look at one of these files you will see what has been set up. The parameters are fairly self-explanatory.

Next, as you can see, the file should not be edited directly. You can make changes by editing the vMX configuration files and re-running the installer, or by using virsh. You can also view this XML file by using virsh's `virsh dumpxml vcp-vmx1` command:

```
mdinham@vmx-day1:/etc/libvirt/qemu$ sudo cat vcp-vmx1.xml
<!--
WARNING: THIS IS AN AUTO-GENERATED FILE. CHANGES TO IT ARE LIKELY TO BE
OVERWRITTEN AND LOST. Changes to this xml configuration should be made using:
  virsh edit vcp-vmx1
or other application using the libvirt API.
-->

<domain type='kvm'>
  <name>vcp-vmx1</name>
  <uuid>660275df-b966-49b3-837a-1785e67c25dd</uuid>
  <memory unit='KiB'>2000000</memory>
  <currentMemory unit='KiB'>2000000</currentMemory>
  <vcpu placement='static'>1</vcpu>
  <cputune>
    <vcpupin vcpu='0' cpuset='0'/>
  </cputune>
  <resource>
    <partition>/machine</partition>
  </resource>
  <sysinfo type='smbios'>
    <bios>
      <entry name='vendor'>Juniper</entry>
    </bios>
    <system>
      <entry name='manufacturer'>VMX</entry>
      <entry name='product'>VM-vcp_vmx1-161-re-0</entry>
      <entry name='version'>0.1.0</entry>
    </system>
  </sysinfo>
  <os>
    <type arch='x86_64' machine='pc-0.13'>hvm</type>
    <boot dev='hd'/>
    <smbios mode='sysinfo'/>
  </os>
  <features>
```

```
    <acpi/>
    <apic/>
    <pae/>
  </features>
  <cpu mode='host-model'>
    <model fallback='allow'/>
    <topology sockets='1' cores='1' threads='1'/>
  </cpu>
  <clock offset='utc'/>
  <on_poweroff>destroy</on_poweroff>
  <on_reboot>restart</on_reboot>
  <on_crash>restart</on_crash>
  <devices>
    <emulator>/usr/bin/qemu-system-x86_64</emulator>
    <disk type='file' device='disk'>
      <driver name='qemu' type='qcow2' cache='directsync'/>
     <source file='/home/mdinham/vmx-15.1F4-3/build/vmx1/images/jinstall64-vmx-15.1F4.15-
domestic.img'/>
     <target dev='hda' bus='ide'/>
      <address type='drive' controller='0' bus='0' target='0' unit='0'/>
    </disk>
    <disk type='file' device='disk'>
      <driver name='qemu' type='qcow2' cache='directsync'/>
      <source file='/home/mdinham/vmx-15.1F4-3/build/vmx1/images/vmxhdd.img'/>
      <target dev='hdb' bus='ide'/>
      <address type='drive' controller='0' bus='0' target='0' unit='1'/>
    </disk>
    <disk type='file' device='disk'>
      <driver name='qemu' type='raw' cache='directsync'/>
      <source file='/home/mdinham/vmx-15.1F4-3/images/metadata_usb.img'/>
      <target dev='sda' bus='usb'/>
    </disk>
    <controller type='usb' index='0'>
      <address type='pci' domain='0x0000' bus='0x00' slot='0x01' function='0x2'/>
    </controller>
    <controller type='ide' index='0'>
      <address type='pci' domain='0x0000' bus='0x00' slot='0x01' function='0x1'/>
    </controller>
    <controller type='pci' index='0' model='pci-root'/>
    <interface type='bridge'>
      <mac address='0a:00:dd:c0:de:0e'/>
      <source bridge='br-ext'/>
      <target dev='vcp_ext-vmx1'/>
      <model type='e1000'/>
      <address type='pci' domain='0x0000' bus='0x00' slot='0x03' function='0x0'/>
    </interface>
    <interface type='bridge'>
      <mac address='52:54:00:46:80:6a'/>
      <source bridge='br-int-vmx1'/>
      <target dev='vcp_int-vmx1'/>
      <model type='virtio'/>
      <address type='pci' domain='0x0000' bus='0x00' slot='0x05' function='0x0'/>
    </interface>
    <serial type='tcp'>
      <source mode='bind' host='127.0.0.1' service='8601'/>
      <protocol type='telnet'/>
      <target port='0'/>
    </serial>
    <console type='tcp'>
      <source mode='bind' host='127.0.0.1' service='8601'/>
```

```
      <protocol type='telnet'/>
      <target type='serial' port='0'/>
    </console>
    <input type='tablet' bus='usb'/>
    <input type='mouse' bus='ps2'/>
    <input type='keyboard' bus='ps2'/>
    <graphics type='vnc' port='-1' autoport='yes' listen='127.0.0.1'>
      <listen type='address' address='127.0.0.1'/>
    </graphics>
    <sound model='ac97'>
      <address type='pci' domain='0x0000' bus='0x00' slot='0x04' function='0x0'/>
    </sound>
    <video>
      <model type='cirrus' vram='16384' heads='1'/>
      <address type='pci' domain='0x0000' bus='0x00' slot='0x02' function='0x0'/>
    </video>
    <memballoon model='virtio'>
      <address type='pci' domain='0x0000' bus='0x00' slot='0x06' function='0x0'/>
    </memballoon>
  </devices>
</domain>
```

If you want to double check the XML configuration for one of the bridges, then again, it's done by looking at the XML directly with virsh. For example, to view `br-ext`:

```
mdinham@vmx-day1:/etc/libvirt/qemu$ sudo virsh net-dumpxml br-ext
<network>
  <name>br-ext</name>
  <uuid>f45f50a5-9940-49d4-a29f-4d23a82cb314</uuid>
  <forward mode='route'/>
  <bridge name='br-ext' stp='on' delay='0'/>
  <mac address='52:54:00:9f:a0:77'/>
  <ip address='192.168.100.200' netmask='255.255.255.0'>
    <dhcp>
      <host mac='0A:00:DD:C0:DE:0E' name='vcp-vmx1' ip='192.168.100.201'/>
      <host mac='0A:00:DD:C0:DE:10' name='vfp-vmx1' ip='192.168.100.202'/>
    </dhcp>
  </ip>
</network>
```

Notice that there is a set of DHCP configurations. This is used to assign the management addresses that you defined in the vMX configuration file. Try consoling in to the VFP and check that everything is working correctly:

```
mdinham@vmx-day1:~/vmx-15.1F4-3$ sudo ./vmx.sh --console vfp vmx1
--
Login Console Port For vfp-vmx1 - 8602
Press Ctrl-] to exit anytime
--
Trying ::1...
Trying 127.0.0.1...
Connected to localhost.
Escape character is '^]'.


Wind River Linux 6.0.0.12 vfp-vmx1 console
```

```
vfp-vmx1 login: root
Password:
root@vfp-vmx1:~# ifconfig ext
ext       Link encap:Ethernet  HWaddr 0a:00:dd:c0:de:10
          inet addr:192.168.100.202  Bcast:192.168.100.255  Mask:255.255.255.0
          inet6 addr: fe80::800:ddff:fec0:de10/64 Scope:Link
          UP BROADCAST RUNNING MULTICAST  MTU:1500  Metric:1
          RX packets:6658 errors:0 dropped:7 overruns:0 frame:0
          TX packets:11 errors:0 dropped:0 overruns:0 carrier:0
          collisions:0 txqueuelen:1000
          RX bytes:752491 (734.8 KiB)  TX bytes:1646 (1.6 KiB)

root@vfp-vmx1:~#
```

Here you can see the IP address assigned to the ext interface is the one specified in the XML configuration for br-ext.

Virsh

Now let's take a look at a running instance of vMX using the CLI tool virsh. First of all, take a look at the VMs running in the Linux KVM:

```
mdinham@vmx-day1:~ sudo virsh list
 Id    Name                           State
----------------------------------------------------
 1     vcp-vmx1                       running
 2     vfp-vmx1                       running
```

Here you can see the two virtual machines, the VCP and the VFP, and notice they are both running. If you want to get some more information on the running VMs, then use the dominfo command:

```
mdinham@vmx-day1:~/vmx-15.1F4-3$ sudo virsh dominfo vcp-vmx1
Id:             1
Name:           vcp-vmx1
UUID:           660275df-b966-49b3-837a-1785e67c25dd
OS Type:        hvm
State:          running
CPU(s):         1
CPU time:       405.3s
Max memory:     2000896 KiB
Used memory:    2000896 KiB
Persistent:     yes
Autostart:      disable
Managed save:   no
Security model: none
Security DOI:   0
```

You can also use virsh to display the interfaces that the vMX has in use by using the domiflist command:

```
mdinham@vmx-day1:~/vmx-15.1F4-3$ sudo virsh domiflist vcp-vmx1
Interface  Type       Source     Model       MAC
-------------------------------------------------------
vcp_ext-vmx1 bridge     br-ext     e1000       0a:00:dd:c0:de:0e
vcp_int-vmx1 bridge     br-int-vmx1 virtio      52:54:00:46:80:6a
```

```
mdinham@vmx-day1:~/vmx-15.1F4-3$ sudo virsh domiflist vfp-vmx1
Interface  Type       Source     Model       MAC
-------------------------------------------------------
vfp_ext-vmx1 bridge    br-ext     virtio      0a:00:dd:c0:de:10
vfp_int-vmx1 bridge    br-int-vmx1 virtio      52:54:00:c4:10:d8
ge-0.0.0-vmx1 network   default    virtio      02:06:0a:0e:ff:f0
```

Here you can see the Linux bridges and interfaces on each VM. As expected, the VCP and VFP have the internal and external bridges set up, and the VFP shows the ge-0/0/0 data interface you created earlier.

Try It Yourself: Using virsh

See what else you can learn about the vMX virtual machines and interface configuration. Run virsh with the `help` option to see what other parameters and configuration can be displayed.

Summary

You should now have all the information on how to build a vMX, manage, and connect to an instance, for lab purposes or otherwise.

Spend some time checking that everything is up and running because you are about to build a simple topology by adding a second vMX instance, which will be connected to the one that you just built!

It's called networking.

Chapter 3

Build a Simple Topology

In this chapter you will extend the single instance topology and create a multi-router topology using two vMXs, and also, logical systems, and then, just to demonstrate the capability of the vMXs, you will go on to configure EVPN on this topology.

Lab Topology

In this lab you will create the following simple topology of four MX routers. You will be able to extend the principles shown here to expand your own topology to be as large and complex as you like. A more detailed topology will be shown in Chapter 4.

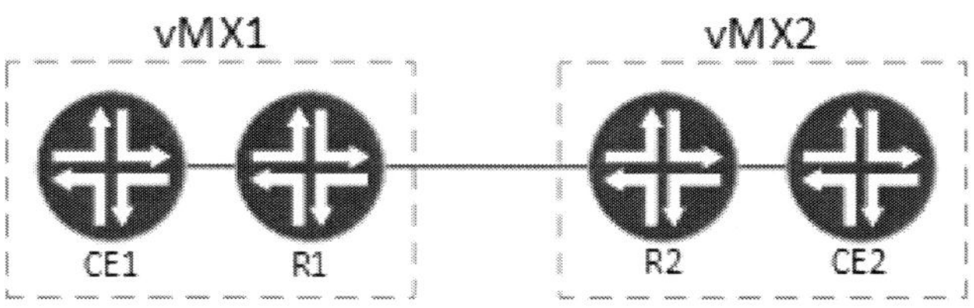

Figure 3.1 Lab Topology

The topology consists of two vMXs running on the same Ubuntu host. You will create CE1 and CE2 as logical system routers.

In the topology you will configure EVPN, however EVPN is unfortunately not supported within a logical system, so R1 and R2 will be the main routers on each vMX and will be your EVPN PEs.

The connectivity between each vMX will be provided via Linux bridges. On each vMX instance you will connect ge-0/0/1 and ge-0/0/2 back-to-back using the Linux bridge, and these interfaces will then be used to provide the interconnection between the main router and the logical system using VLANs. Another option would be to use logical tunnel interfaces.

The ge-0/0/3 interface on vMX1 and vMX2 will be interconnected using a Linux virtio bridge on the host.

Set Up a Second Instance of vMX

First things first, so let's get the second instance of vMX running. If you remember from Chapter 2, there is a configuration file for a vMX instance. Running a second vMX instance on a host is no different, and the second instance of vMX has its own settings file.

You will need to copy vMX1's configuration file and use that as the basis for vMX2. If you've not already done so, it's time to SSH in to the KVM host and change to the directory location where you installed the vMX:

```
mdinham@vmx-day1:~/vmx-15.1F4-3$ cd config/
mdinham@vmx-day1:~/vmx-15.1F4-3/config$ cp vmx.conf vmx2.conf
```

Now let's have a look at the settings to be changed in vmx2.conf

When running multiple instances of vMX on the same host, each vMX instance needs to be configured with a unique identifier. Modify the configuration in vmx2.conf – the vMX identifier should be changed to *vmx2*.

This lab topology makes use of the same host management interface for both vMX1 and vMX2 and no changes need to be made to the images:

```
HOST:
    identifier               : vmx2   # Maximum 4 characters
    host-management-interface : eth0
    routing-engine-image      : "/home/mdinham/vmx-15.1F4-3/images/jinstall64-vmx-15.1F4.15-
domestic.img"
    routing-engine-hdd       : "/home/mdinham/vmx-15.1F4-3/images/vmxhdd.img"
    forwarding-engine-image   : "/home/mdinham/vmx-15.1F4-3/images/vFPC-20151203.img"
```

The external bridge can be used by both vMX1 and vMX2 so no need to change this setting. Remember that this is used to bridge the management interfaces on the vMX to the host management interface defined above:

```
BRIDGES:
     - type  : external
       name  : br-ext                    # Max 10 characters
```

For the VCP and VFP you will need to make some changes to the console port, the management IP address, and the MAC address.

The default MAC addresses used in the configuration file are taken from the locally administered MAC address ranges, so it is no problem to choose your own address from this range, but take care not to overlap with the vMX1. Also, set a console port number and management IP address that will not overlap with vMX1:

```
#vRE VM parameters
CONTROL_PLANE:
    vcpus       : 1
    memory-mb   : 2048
    console_port: 8603

    interfaces  :
      - type      : static
        ipaddr    : 192.168.100.203
        macaddr   : "0A:00:DD:C0:DE:0F"

---
#vPFE VM parameters
FORWARDING_PLANE:
    memory-mb   : 8192
    vcpus       : 3
    console_port: 8604
    device-type : virtio

    interfaces  :
      - type      : static
        ipaddr    : 192.168.100.204
        macaddr   : "0A:00:DD:C0:DE:11"
```

CAUTION If you are tight on resources in your lab I completed the labs in this book running Ubuntu as a nested VM on my MacBook. I allocated 4GB to the forwarding plane (which is below the Juniper recommendation of 8GB for 15.1) and the forwarding plane loaded. 4GB could be fine for your lab purposes depending on the features and version of vMX that you are using. 1GB should be the absolute minimum on the control plane. Please don't do this in a production environment because it is not a Juniper supported configuration and if something goes wrong, JTAC won't help you!

You should now uncomment ge-0/0/0 through ge-0/0/3 and again update the MAC addresses to ensure there's no clash with the vMX1:

```
---
#Interfaces
JUNOS_DEVICES:
   - interface            : ge-0/0/0
     mac-address          : "02:06:0A:0E:FF:F4"
     description          : "ge-0/0/0 interface"

   - interface            : ge-0/0/1
     mac-address          : "02:06:0A:0E:FF:F5"
     description          : "ge-0/0/0 interface"

   - interface            : ge-0/0/2
```

```
    mac-address          : "02:06:0A:0E:FF:F6"
    description          : "ge-0/0/0 interface"

  - interface            : ge-0/0/3
    mac-address          : "02:06:0A:0E:FF:F7"
    description          : "ge-0/0/0 interface"
```

Once you have saved the configuration file, vMX2 is ready to be built. The same orchestration script that you used to create vMX1 is again used for vMX2, but this time you will need to specify an additional option to point the script at vMX2's configuration file.

CAUTION Each time you use vmx.sh to perform stop/start operations on vMX2, you must specify the configuration file for vMX2. Take care not to accidentally perform a stop operation on the wrong vMX! In a production environment, you should not use the default configuration file locations. This ensures that you must always specify a non-default configuration every time you execute the vmx.sh script.

Now enter the following command, the script will create the new vMX instance and will automatically start it for you:

```
mdinham@vmx-day1:~/vmx-15.1F4-3$ sudo ./vmx.sh -lv --install --cfg config/vmx2.conf
==================================================
    Welcome to VMX
==================================================
Date..............................................02/23/16 14:18:10
VMX Identifier....................................vmx2
Config file......................................./home/mdinham/vmx-15.1F4-3/config/vmx2.
conf
Build Directory.................................../home/mdinham/vmx-15.1F4-3/build/vmx2
Environment file................................../home/mdinham/vmx-15.1F4-3/env/ubuntu_
virtio.env
Junos Device Type.................................virtio
Initialize scripts................................[OK]
Copy images to build directory....................[OK]
==================================================
    VMX Environment Setup Completed
==================================================

<OUTPUT REMOVED>

==================================================
    System Setup Completed
==================================================
Generate libvirt files............................[OK]
Sleep 2 secs......................................[OK]
Find configured management interface..............eth0
Find existing management gateway..................br-ext
Check if eth0 is already enslaved to br-ext.......[Yes]
Create br-int-vmx2................................[OK]
Start br-int-vmx2.................................[OK]
Check and start default bridge....................[OK]
Define vcp-vmx2...................................[OK]
Define vfp-vmx2...................................[OK]
Wait 2 secs.......................................[OK]
```

```
Start vcp-vmx2....................................[OK]
Start vfp-vmx2....................................[OK]
Wait 2 secs.......................................[OK]
==================================================
    VMX Bringup Completed
==================================================
Check if br-ext is created........................[Created]
Check if br-int-vmx2 is created...................[Created]
Check if VM vcp-vmx2 is running...................[Running]
Check if VM vfp-vmx2 is running...................[Running]
Check if tap interface vcp_ext-vmx2 exists........[OK]
Check if tap interface vcp_int-vmx2 exists........[OK]
Check if tap interface vfp_ext-vmx2 exists........[OK]
Check if tap interface vfp_int-vmx2 exists........[OK]
==================================================
    VMX Status Verification Completed.
==================================================
Log file..........................................
    /home/mdinham/vmx-15.1F4-3/build/vmx2/logs/vmx_1456237090.log
==================================================
    Thankyou for using VMX
==================================================
```

You are now ready to connect to the console on vMX2. This is done the same way for vMX1 and vMX2. You simply reference the correct vMX instance when running the script. If you wish, now would be a good time to configure SSH access to vMX2:

```
mdinham@vmx-day1:~/vmx-15.1F4-3$ sudo ./vmx.sh --console vcp vmx2
--
Login Console Port For vcp-vmx2 - 8603
Press Ctrl-] to exit anytime
--
Trying ::1...
Trying 127.0.0.1...
Connected to localhost.
Escape character is '^]'.

Amnesiac (ttyd0)

login:
```

Now, check the configured Linux bridges again:

```
mdinham@vmx-day1:~/vmx-15.1F4-3$ brctl show
bridge name     bridge id               STP enabled     interfaces
br-ext          8000.000c29510c44       yes             br-ext-nic
                                                        eth0
                                                        vcp_ext-vmx1
                                                        vcp_ext-vmx2
                                                        vfp_ext-vmx1
                                                        vfp_ext-vmx2
br-int-vmx1     8000.5254008f5d25       yes             br-int-vmx1-nic
                                                        vcp_int-vmx1
                                                        vfp_int-vmx1
br-int-vmx2     8000.525400809ad8       yes             br-int-vmx2-nic
                                                        vcp_int-vmx2
                                                        vfp_int-vmx2
```

You can see that the vMX script automatically created another internal bridge named `br-int-vmx2`. This time the internal bridge is present to enable the VCP and VFP communication for vMX2. The external bridge (management bridge) is shared by all vMX management interfaces.

There are a couple of error messages that you might see if things didn't go well during the deployment of vMX. For instance, the next example shows that the console ports assigned to vMX1 and vMX2 are the same:

```
Start vcp-vmx2...................................[Failed]
error: Failed to start domain vcp-vmx2
error: internal error: process exited while connecting to monitor:
2015-12-16T21:09:18.408436Z qemu-system-x86_64: -chardev socket,id=charserial0,host=127.0.0.
1,port=8601,telnet,server,nowait: Failed to bind socket: Address already in use
2015-12-16T21:09:18.408496Z qemu-system-x86_64: -chardev socket,id=charserial0,host=127.0.0.
1,port=8601,telnet,server,nowait:
```

This next error message shows that there isn't enough system memory to start the VCP virtual machine:

```
Start vfp-vmx2...................................[Failed]
error: Failed to start domain vfp-vmx2
error: internal error: early end of file from monitor: possible problem:
CPU feature invtsc not found
CPU feature invtsc not found
CPU feature invtsc not found
file_ram_alloc: can't mmap RAM pages: Cannot allocate memory
```

If you remember when vMX1 was deployed in Chapter 2, only one `ge-` interface was configured. Before going any further in this lab, you will need to add the additional interfaces to vMX1. But first of all use the libvirt `virsh` CLI command to compare vMX1 with vMX2.

Use the `list` command to show the VMs (domains) that are configured. You can then use the `domiflist` command to show all the configured interfaces. You are interested in the forwarding plane interfaces, so you will need to query the correct domain ID, here 5 and 7:

```
mdinham@vmx-day1:~/vmx-15.1F4-3$ sudo virsh list
 Id    Name                           State
----------------------------------------------------
 4     vcp-vmx1                       running
 5     vfp-vmx1                       running
 6     vcp-vmx2                       running
 7     vfp-vmx2                       running

mdinham@vmx-day1:~/vmx-15.1F4-3$ sudo virsh domiflist 5
Interface  Type       Source     Model       MAC
-------------------------------------------------------
vfp_ext-vmx1 bridge     br-ext     virtio      0a:00:dd:c0:de:10
vfp_int-vmx1 bridge     br-int-vmx1 virtio      52:54:00:96:39:ea
ge-0.0.0-vmx1 network    default    virtio      02:06:0a:0e:ff:f0

mdinham@vmx-day1:~/vmx-15.1F4-3$ sudo virsh domiflist 7
```

```
Interface   Type          Source      Model       MAC
-------------------------------------------------------
vfp_ext-vmx2 bridge      br-ext      virtio      0a:00:dd:c0:de:11
vfp_int-vmx2 bridge      br-int-vmx2 virtio     52:54:00:42:f7:c1
ge-0.0.0-vmx2 network     default    virtio      02:06:0a:0e:ff:f4
ge-0.0.1-vmx2 network     default    virtio      02:06:0a:0e:ff:f5
ge-0.0.2-vmx2 network     default    virtio      02:06:0a:0e:ff:f6
ge-0.0.3-vmx2 network     default    virtio      02:06:0a:0e:ff:f7
```

As you can see, this `domiflist` command has confirmed that vMX1 is missing the interface. Let's now add these interfaces to vMX1.

Edit the configuration file (config/vmx.conf) and uncomment all four ge interfaces, then save the file:

```
---
#Interfaces
JUNOS_DEVICES:
   - interface            : ge-0/0/0
     mac-address          : "02:06:0A:0E:FF:F0"
     description          : "ge-0/0/0 interface"

   - interface            : ge-0/0/1
     mac-address          : "02:06:0A:0E:FF:F1"
     description          : "ge-0/0/0 interface"

   - interface            : ge-0/0/2
     mac-address          : "02:06:0A:0E:FF:F2"
     description          : "ge-0/0/0 interface"

   - interface            : ge-0/0/3
     mac-address          : "02:06:0A:0E:FF:F3"
     description          : "ge-0/0/0 interface"
```

Just saving the file will not make any changes to a running instance of vMX. You need to stop the running instance of vMX1, and then redeploy the instance:

1. Connect to the console on vMX1's VCP and stop Junos. Use the `request system halt` command to gracefully shut down the Junos software.

2. Stop the running instance (`sudo ./vmx.sh --stop`)

3. Re-deploy vMX1 (`sudo ./vmx.sh --install`)

vMX1 will now be restarted with the additional interfaces. Check that this is the case with `virsh`. Note the domain ID will have changed because the vMX instance has been redeployed:

```
mdinham@vmx-day1:~/vmx-15.1F4-3$ sudo virsh list
 Id    Name                           State
----------------------------------------------------
 6     vcp-vmx2                       running
 7     vfp-vmx2                       running
 8     vcp-vmx1                       running
 9     vfp-vmx1                       running

mdinham@vmx-day1:~/vmx-15.1F4-3$ sudo virsh domiflist 9
```

```
Interface  Type       Source     Model       MAC
-------------------------------------------------------
vfp_ext-vmx1 bridge     br-ext     virtio      0a:00:dd:c0:de:10
vfp_int-vmx1 bridge     br-int-vmx1 virtio      52:54:00:77:79:82
ge-0.0.0-vmx1 network    default    virtio      02:06:0a:0e:ff:f0
ge-0.0.1-vmx1 network    default    virtio      02:06:0a:0e:ff:f1
ge-0.0.2-vmx1 network    default    virtio      02:06:0a:0e:ff:f2
ge-0.0.3-vmx1 network    default    virtio      02:06:0a:0e:ff:f3
```

It's now time to connect vMX1 and vMX2 and build your simple topology.

Link Two vMXs with Virtio

For the Ethernet connectivity to the vMX you will be using KVM virtio paravirtualisation.

Virtio bindings are flexible and can be used to map multiple vMX instances to a physical host interface, or to connect vMX instances or vMX interfaces together, which you'll be doing here. Linux bridges are used to stitch everything together.

A Linux bridge is a way to connect two or more Ethernet segments in software. Think of it like a virtual network switch. Packets are forwarded based on MAC address and both untagged and 802.1q tagged frames are supported.

At this point both vMX1 and vMX2 are running, but you need to create the virtio bindings to enable the communication between each vMX.

For both vMX1 and vMX2 this is done in the same configuration file – `config/vmx-junosdev.conf`. The goal is to connect interfaces ge-0/0/1 to ge-0/0/2 back-to-back on each vMX, and link together the vMX instances using ge-0/0/3 on each vMX.

Create a link between vMX1 interfaces ge-0/0/1 and ge-0/0/2:

```
- link_name  : vmx1_link_ls
  endpoint_1 :
    - type        : junos_dev
      vm_name     : vmx1
      dev_name    : ge-0/0/1
  endpoint_2 :
    - type        : junos_dev
      vm_name     : vmx1
      dev_name    : ge-0/0/2
```

The same is done for vMX2:

```
- link_name  : vmx2_link_ls
  endpoint_1 :
    - type        : junos_dev
      vm_name     : vmx2
```

```
        dev_name    : ge-0/0/1
    endpoint_2 :
      - type        : junos_dev
        vm_name     : vmx2
        dev_name    : ge-0/0/2
```

Finally, create a link between ge-0/0/3 on vMX1 and vMX2. You could use the same technique as shown above, but what if you wanted to connect more than two vMXs on the same Ethernet segment? That would be done like this, with an additional bridge being defined and shared by each vMX:

```
  - link_name  : bridge_vmx_12
    endpoint_1 :
      - type        : junos_dev
        vm_name     : vmx1
        dev_name    : ge-0/0/3
    endpoint_2 :
      - type        : bridge_dev
        dev_name    : bridge_vmx12

  - link_name  : bridge_vmx_12
    endpoint_1 :
      - type        : junos_dev
        vm_name     : vmx2
        dev_name    : ge-0/0/3
    endpoint_2 :
      - type        : bridge_dev
        dev_name    : bridge_vmx12
```

Again the orchestration script vmx.sh is used to create the device bindings:

```
mdinham@vmx-day1:~/vmx-15.1F4-3$ sudo ./vmx.sh --bind-dev
Checking package ethtool.........................[OK]
Numa node for eth1...............................-1
Cores servicing numa node -1.....................
Pid of vfp-vmx1..................................12222
Bind Link vmx1_link_ls(ge-0.0.1-vmx1, ge-0.0.2-vmx1)
[OK]
Bind Link vmx2_link_ls(ge-0.0.1-vmx2, ge-0.0.2-vmx2)
[OK]
Bind Bridge port bridge_vmx12(ge-0.0.3-vmx1)......[OK]
Bind Bridge port bridge_vmx12(ge-0.0.3-vmx2)......[OK]
```

Now let's look at what bridges were created:

```
mdinham@vmx-day1:~/vmx-15.1F4-3$  brctl show
bridge name     bridge id               STP enabled     interfaces

br-ext          8000.000c29510c44       yes             br-ext-nic
                                                        eth0
                                                        vcp_ext-vmx1
                                                        vcp_ext-vmx2
                                                        vfp_ext-vmx1
                                                        vfp_ext-vmx2
br-int-vmx1     8000.5254008f5d25       yes             br-int-vmx1-nic
                                                        vcp_int-vmx1
```

```
                                                        vfp_int-vmx1
br-int-vmx2      8000.525400809ad8       yes            br-int-vmx2-nic
                                                        vcp_int-vmx2
                                                        vfp_int-vmx2
bridge_vmx12     8000.fe060a0efff3       no             ge-0.0.3-vmx1
                                                        ge-0.0.3-vmx2
vmx2_link_ls     8000.fe060a0efff5       no             ge-0.0.1-vmx2
                                                        ge-0.0.2-vmx2
vmx1_link_ls     8000.fe060a0efff1       no             ge-0.0.1-vmx1
                                                        ge-0.0.2-vmx1
```

Here's a description for each bridge:

- `br-ext` The external bridge for management traffic
- `br-int-vmx1` The internal bridge for vMX1 RE to PFE traffic
- `br-int-vmx2` The internal bridge for vMX2 RE to PFE traffic
- `bridge_vmx12` Enables the communication between ge-0/0/3 on vMX1 and vMX2
- `virbr0` This default KVM bridge is unused as all vMX interfaces are defined (not shown above)
- `vmx1_link_ls` Connects ge-0/0/1 and ge-0/0/2 on vMX1
- `vmx2_link_ls` Connects ge-0/0/1 and ge-0/0/2 on vMX2

At this point vMX1 and vMX2 are ready to be configured. What better way to test your two vMXs than a quick lab build!

EVPN Lab

EVPN is defined in RFC7432. It provides a number of enhancements over VPLS, particularly as MAC address learning now occurs in the control plane and is advertised between PEs using an MP-BGP MAC route. Compared to VPLS, which uses data plane flooding to learn MAC addresses, this BGP-based approach enables EVPN to limit the flooding of unknown unicast. MAC addresses are now being routed, which in multihomed scenarios enables all active links to be utilized. Neat stuff.

MORE? See *Day One: Using Ethernet VPNs for Data Center Interconnect* at http://www.juniper.net/us/en/training/jnbooks/day-one/proof-concept-labs/using-ethernet-vpns/.

Lab Topology

You will now create a topology that makes use of the virtio bindings that were already created earlier in this chapter. To recap, ge-0/0/1 and ge-0/0/2 are connected back-to-back on vMX1 and vMX2. Then vMX1 and vMX2 are connected via ge-0/0/3. In terms of this topology:

- R1 ge-0/0/3 connects to R2 ge-0/0/3
- CE1 ge-0/0/2 (VLAN 34) connects to R1 ge-0/0/1 (VLAN 34)
- CE2 ge-0/0/2 (VLAN 34) connects to R2 ge-0/0/1 (VLAN 34)

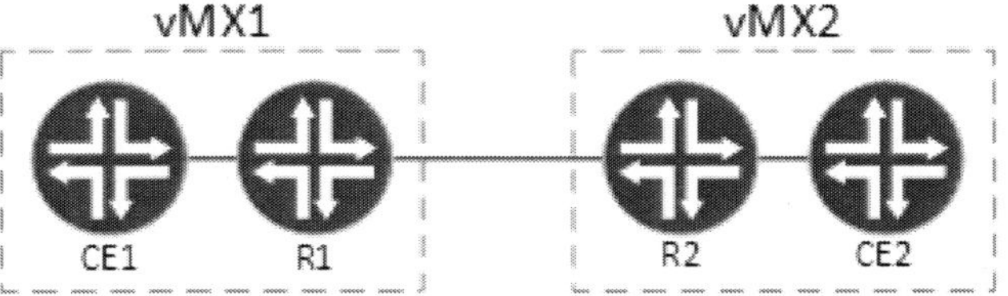

Figure 3.2 This Lab's Topology

R1 and R2 represent your core routers and as such will be running MPLS. You will configure EVPN on R1 and R2 and use EVPN to create a Layer 2 connection between CE1 and CE2.

You can consider this lab a success if CE1 and CE2 view each other as directly adjacent and if you are able to ping between CE1 and CE2.

NOTE This *Day One* book is about building up your lab topology using vMX, so detail on EVPN will be at a high level. If you would like to know more about EVPN then check out the Day One book previously cited at http://www.juniper.net/us/en/training/jnbooks/day-one/proof-concept-labs/using-ethernet-vpns/.

Lab Configuration

If you have not already applied a trial license to vMX2 you should refer back to Chapter 2 and apply a trial license now before continuing any further.

First, let's apply a base configuration to R1 and R2 and then test the connectivity. In the base configuration, R1 and R2 should use OSPF as the IGP. Also:

- You will need MPLS so enable family MPLS and LDP on interface ge-0/0/3.
- For R1 use a loopback IP of 1.1.1.1/32 and ge-0/0/3.0 as 192.168.12.1/30.

- For R2 use a loopback IP of 2.2.2.2/32 and ge-0/0/3.0 as 192.168.12.2/30.

On vMX1:

```
set system host-name R1
set interfaces ge-0/0/3 unit 0 family inet address 192.168.12.1/30
set interfaces ge-0/0/3 unit 0 family mpls
set interfaces lo0 unit 0 family inet address 1.1.1.1/32
set routing-options router-id 1.1.1.1
set protocols mpls interface ge-0/0/3.0
set protocols ospf area 0.0.0.0 interface lo0.0 passive
set protocols ospf area 0.0.0.0 interface ge-0/0/3.0
set protocols ldp interface ge-0/0/3.0
```

On vMX2:

```
set system host-name R2
set interfaces ge-0/0/3 unit 0 family inet address 192.168.12.2/30
set interfaces ge-0/0/3 unit 0 family mpls
set interfaces lo0 unit 0 family inet address 2.2.2.2/32
set routing-options router-id 2.2.2.2
set protocols mpls interface ge-0/0/3.0
set protocols ospf area 0.0.0.0 interface lo0.0 passive
set protocols ospf area 0.0.0.0 interface ge-0/0/3.0
set protocols ldp interface ge-0/0/3.0
```

Don't forget to set a password for the root account before you commit the configuration:

```
set system root-authentication plain-text-password
```

Next check the status of the OSPF neighbors. If everything is up you should be able to ping between the two loopback addresses:

```
root@R1> show ospf neighbor
Address          Interface              State     ID               Pri  Dead
192.168.12.2     ge-0/0/3.0             Full      2.2.2.2          128    39

root@R1> ping 2.2.2.2 rapid source 1.1.1.1
PING 2.2.2.2 (2.2.2.2): 56 data bytes
!!!!!
--- 2.2.2.2 ping statistics ---
5 packets transmitted, 5 packets received, 0% packet loss
round-trip min/avg/max/stddev = 1.018/1.299/1.685/0.223 ms
```

Now that you have reachability between R1 and R2 you can go ahead and add the required base configuration for EVPN.

NOTE Unfortunately, EVPN is not supported within a logical system, which is why you will need to configure EVPN on the main routers.

You will now configure MP-BGP making sure to activate the `evpn signaling` MP-BGP address family. As this EVPN configuration is Layer 2 only, the `inet-vpn unicast` MP-BGP address family is optional. To configure the iBGP peering between R1 and R2:

- Use AS65000 as your Autonomous System
- Configure the BGP peering between each Loopback address

On R1 (vMX1):

```
set routing-options autonomous-system 65000
set protocols bgp group internal type internal
set protocols bgp group internal local-address 1.1.1.1
set protocols bgp group internal family inet-vpn unicast
set protocols bgp group internal family evpn signaling
set protocols bgp group internal neighbor 2.2.2.2
```

On R2 (vMX2):

```
set routing-options autonomous-system 65000
set protocols bgp group internal type internal
set protocols bgp group internal local-address 2.2.2.2
set protocols bgp group internal family inet-vpn unicast
set protocols bgp group internal family evpn signaling
set protocols bgp group internal neighbor 1.1.1.1
```

Make sure that the neighborship is established, but of course you will not see any routes received or advertised at this point:

```
root@R1> show bgp summary
Groups: 1 Peers: 1 Down peers: 0
Table          Tot Paths  Act Paths Suppressed    History Damp State    Pending
bgp.l3vpn.0
                       0          0          0          0          0          0
bgp.evpn.0
                       0          0          0          0          0          0
Peer                     AS      InPkt     OutPkt    OutQ   Flaps Last Up/
Dwn State|#Active/Received/Accepted/Damped...
2.2.2.2               65000          4          4       0       0          32 Establ
  bgp.l3vpn.0: 0/0/0/0
  bgp.evpn.0: 0/0/0/0
```

Logical Systems

The configuration gets a little more complicated here, because you need to create CE1 and CE2 as logical system routers on each vMX.

Remember that ge-0/0/1 and ge0/0/2 have been connected back-to-back by the virtio bridge. Use ge-0/0/1 as the interface on R1/R2, and ge-0/0/2 as the interfaces on the logical system routers CE1/CE2.

Configure your topology as follows:

- Create a logical system named *CE1* on R1, assigning interface ge-0/0/2. Configure the IP 192.168.34.3/29 on ge-0/0/2. Use a VLAN ID of 34.
- Create a logical system named *CE2* on R2, assigning interface ge-0/0/2. Configure the IP 192.168.34.4/29 on ge-0/0/2. Use a VLAN ID of 34.

In Chapter 4 you will see much more on logical system routers.

On R1 (vMX1):

```
set logical-systems CE1 interfaces ge-0/0/2 unit 34 vlan-id 34
set logical-systems CE1 interfaces ge-0/0/2 unit 34 family inet address 192.168.34.3/29
set interfaces ge-0/0/2 vlan-tagging
```

On R2 (vMX2):

```
set logical-systems CE2 interfaces ge-0/0/2 unit 34 vlan-id 34
set logical-systems CE2 interfaces ge-0/0/2 unit 34 family inet address 192.168.34.4/29
set interfaces ge-0/0/2 vlan-tagging
```

Working with these logical systems is simple and commands can be entered in a couple of ways. Configuration can also be entered directly when the CLI is set to a logical system. Here are two ways to ping CE1's own interface:

```
root@R1> set cli logical-system CE1
logical system: CE1

root@R1:CE1> ping 192.168.34.3 rapid
PING 192.168.34.3 (192.168.34.3): 56 data bytes
!!!!!
--- 192.168.34.3 ping statistics ---
5 packets transmitted, 5 packets received, 0% packet loss
round-trip min/avg/max/stddev = 0.005/0.010/0.020/0.006 ms

root@R1:CE1> clear cli logical-system
Cleared default logical system

root@R1> ping logical-system CE1 192.168.34.3 rapid
PING 192.168.34.3 (192.168.34.3): 56 data bytes
!!!!!
--- 192.168.34.3 ping statistics ---
5 packets transmitted, 5 packets received, 0% packet loss
round-trip min/avg/max/stddev = 0.004/0.008/0.017/0.005 ms
```

Clearly at this point CE1 and CE2 will not be able to ping each other because you need to use EVPN to provide the Layer 2 connectivity.

Completing the EVPN Configuration

You are now going to configure the EVPN VLAN-based service. This requires a separate EVI per VLAN. An EVI is an EVPN instance spanning across the PEs participating in a particular EVPN.

There isn't too much to the configuration:

- On R1 and R2 configure the interface-facing CE1 (ge-0/0/1) to support VLAN tagging and with `flexible-ethernet-services` `encapsulation`. You will also need to configure unit 34 with the correct `vlan-id` and `vlan-bridge` encapsulation.

- You will also need to define the EVPN routing instance itself. Interface ge-0/0/1.34 (the interface facing the CE router) is added to the EVPN instance.

Here is the sample configuration for R1 and R2:

```
set interfaces ge-0/0/1 flexible-vlan-tagging
set interfaces ge-0/0/1 encapsulation flexible-ethernet-services
set interfaces ge-0/0/1 unit 34 encapsulation vlan-bridge
set interfaces ge-0/0/1 unit 34 vlan-id 34
set routing-instances EVPN34 instance-type evpn
set routing-instances EVPN34 vlan-id 34
set routing-instances EVPN34 interface ge-0/0/1.34
set routing-instances EVPN34 route-distinguisher 1.1.1.1:1
set routing-instances EVPN34 vrf-target target:34:34
set routing-instances EVPN34 protocols evpn
```

Verification

At this point the configuration of EVPN is complete, so let's verify that everything is working as expected. On the EVPN PE routers, check that the routes are being received in BGP:

```
root@R1> show bgp summary
Groups: 1 Peers: 1 Down peers: 0
Table          Tot Paths  Act Paths Suppressed    History Damp State    Pending
bgp.l3vpn.0
                       0          0          0          0          0          0
bgp.evpn.0
                       1          1          0          0          0          0
Peer                     AS      InPkt     OutPkt    OutQ   Flaps Last Up/
Dwn State|#Active/Received/Accepted/Damped...
2.2.2.2               65000         83         55       0       0       20:34 Establ
  bgp.l3vpn.0: 0/0/0/0
  bgp.evpn.0: 1/1/1/0
  EVPN34.evpn.0: 1/1/1/0
  __default_evpn__.evpn.0: 0/0/0/0
```

That looks good – one route received. As previously mentioned, this configuration is Layer 2 only, so table *bgp.l3vpn.0* remains empty.

Can CE1 and CE2 now ping each other? Let's see:

```
root@R1> set cli logical-system CE1
Logical system: CE1

root@R1:CE1> ping 192.168.34.4 rapid
PING 192.168.34.4 (192.168.34.4): 56 data bytes
!!!!!
```

```
--- 192.168.34.4 ping statistics ---
5 packets transmitted, 5 packets received, 0% packet loss
round-trip min/avg/max/stddev = 2.432/49.696/200.211/76.672 ms

root@R1:CE1> show arp
MAC Address       Address         Name               Interface             Flags
02:06:0a:0e:ff:f6 192.168.34.4    192.168.34.4       ge-0/0/2.34           none
```

Looks good! Notice that the CE2 MAC address is in CE1's ARP table.

Now for a little more detail on what the EVPN PEs are seeing. Connect back to R1. You should be able to see the MAC addresses in the BGP table, the directly-attached device, but also the device attached to R3:

```
root@R1> show route table EVPN34.evpn.0

EVPN34.evpn.0: 4 destinations, 4 routes (4 active, 0 holddown, 0 hidden)
+ = Active Route, - = Last Active, * = Both

2:1.1.1.1:1::34::02:06:0a:0e:ff:f2/304
                   *[EVPN/170] 00:01:52
                      Indirect
2:1.1.1.1:1::34::02:06:0a:0e:ff:f6/304
                   *[BGP/170] 00:01:52, localpref 100, from 2.2.2.2
                      AS path: I, validation-state: unverified
                    > to 192.168.12.2 via ge-0/0/3.0
3:1.1.1.1:1::34::1.1.1.1/304
                   *[EVPN/170] 00:04:04
                      Indirect
3:1.1.1.1:1::34::2.2.2.2/304
                   *[BGP/170] 00:02:54, localpref 100, from 2.2.2.2
                      AS path: I, validation-state: unverified
                    > to 192.168.12.2 via ge-0/0/3.0
```

If you would like to view the compete EVPN database and MAC table, it is viewable by using the `show evpn database` command:

```
root@R1> show evpn database
Instance: EVPN34
VLAN  MAC address        Active source                  Timestamp        IP address
34    02:06:0a:0e:ff:f2  ge-0/0/1.34                    Feb 23 15:03:42
34    02:06:0a:0e:ff:f6  2.2.2.2                        Feb 23 15:05:24

root@R1> show evpn mac-table

MAC flags       (S -static MAC, D -dynamic MAC, L -locally learned, C -Control MAC
    O -OVSDB MAC, SE -Statistics enabled, NM -Non configured MAC, R -Remote PE MAC)

Routing instance : EVPN34
 Bridging domain : __EVPN34__, VLAN : 34
   MAC                MAC      Logical          NH      RTR
   address            flags    interface        Index   ID
   02:06:0a:0e:ff:f2  D        ge-0/0/1.34
   02:06:0a:0e:ff:f6  DC                        1048575 1048575
```

You can also check that local MAC addresses are being advertised from R1 to R2:

```
root@R1> show route advertising-protocol bgp 2.2.2.2

EVPN34.evpn.0: 4 destinations, 4 routes (4 active, 0 holddown, 0 hidden)
  Prefix                  Nexthop              MED     Lclpref    AS path
  2:1.1.1.1:1::34::02:06:0a:0e:ff:f2/304
*                         Self                         100        I
  3:1.1.1.1:1::34::1.1.1.1/304
*                         Self                         100        I
```

You can also view detailed information about the EVPN routing instance. There is some useful information here, for example, the total number of MAC addresses:

```
root@R1> show evpn instance EVPN34 extensive
Instance: EVPN34
  Route Distinguisher: 1.1.1.1:1
  VLAN ID: 34
  Per-instance MAC route label: 299808
  MAC database status                Local  Remote
    Total MAC addresses:                 1       1
    Default gateway MAC addresses:       0       0
  Number of local interfaces: 1 (1 up)
    Interface name  ESI                            Mode             Status
    ge-0/0/1.34     00:00:00:00:00:00:00:00:00:00  single-homed     Up
  Number of IRB interfaces: 0 (0 up)
  Number of bridge domains: 1
    VLAN ID  Intfs / up    Mode             MAC sync  IM route label
    34           1   1     Extended         Enabled   299872
  Number of neighbors: 1
    2.2.2.2
      Received routes
        MAC address advertisement:              1
        MAC+IP address advertisement:           0
        Inclusive multicast:                    1
        Ethernet auto-discovery:                0
  Number of ethernet segments: 0
```

Try It Yourself: Monitor the Traffic Going Between the Two Logical System Routers

As you have used Linux bridges to interconnect the logical system routers you can use tcpdump on the Linux host to monitor traffic between each logical system router. This is achieved by monitoring the Linux bridge:

```
sudo tcpdump -i vmx1_link_ls -n
```

Summary

In this chapter you discovered how simple it is to deploy and interconnect multiple vMXs on the same Linux host. And of course you just built a topology of four logical routers on the two vMXs and used EVPN to demonstrate the extensive capability of vMX.

Time to rock. Let's scale it.

Chapter 4

Scaling Your vMX Topology

Now let's scale your lab topology. There are a couple of options here, depending on your own preference and the amount of capacity that you have to spare on your KVM host.

The obvious option for scaling a lab using vMX routers is simply to run more vMX instances on the same host. If you have the hardware available, then this is certainly a good choice. Using the principles you've learned throughout this book, you can simply add more vMX instances and connect interfaces together using virtio bindings and Linux bridges. This is a very flexible and simple way to build a large topology.

But what if your lab hardware specification is not enough to run several vMXs on the same host? Well you can use fewer vMXs and make extensive use of virtual routers or logical systems as shown in Chapter 3. In this chapter you will scale out our topology of two vMXs using logical systems. With just two vMXs and use of logical systems, you could create a topology of thirty routers.

Just for fun, a Linux VM will be added to the topology and it will be configured as a CE, but also with a BGP route server installed.

Let's get started.

Scale Your vMX - Topology

You will need to create three VMs to complete this lab, two vMX instances and an Ubuntu Linux virtual machine as shown in Figure 4.1. And Table 4.1 lists how each VM interface will be configured.

Figure 4.1 Chapter 4 Topology

Table 4.1 Lab Interface Configuration

VM	Interface	Connects to	Note
CE1	eth1	vMX1 ge-0/0/0	
vMX1	ge-0/0/0	CE1 eth1	
vMX1	ge-0/0/1	vMX1 ge-0/0/2	Used for logical system communication
vMX1	ge-0/0/2	vMX1 ge-0/0/1	Used for logical system communication
vMX1	ge-0/0/3	vMX2 ge-0/0/3	Used for vMX instance communication
vMX2	ge-0/0/3	vMX1 ge-0/0/3	Used for vMX instance communication

Communication between logical systems can be done in a couple of ways:

- Ethernet Interfaces and VLANs
- Logical Tunnel interfaces

In Chapter 3, communication between logical systems was accomplished using Ethernet interfaces and VLANs. Two vMX interfaces were connected back-to-back using virtio and Linux bridges to link the interfaces together. One end of the link was placed in one logical system, and the other end was placed in a different logical system.

The same thing can also be accomplished using logical tunnel interfaces. This simply creates a set of logical point-to-point interfaces on the vMX. One end of the link is placed in one logical system, and the other end of the point-to-point is placed in a different logical system. As with a physical interface, you can run dynamic routing protocols over the tunnel if you wish. Logical tunnels are a really flexible way to leak routes between routing instances or logical systems. They've probably helped you out a few times!

In this lab, vMX1 will use Ethernet interfaces to join the logical systems and vMX2 will use logical tunnels to join the logical systems.

Logical Topology

Figure 4.2 illustrates the topology you will create. The network will run OSPF as the IGP – and MPLS of course – but this time it's RSVP signaled. The goal is to enable VPLS over this topology and use VPLS to link CE1 and CE2. You could do a simple Layer 2 circuit point-to-point link, but what if your customer tells you they expect to add additional sites later and these sites all need to be directly reachable at Layer 2? So VPLS it is. EVPN would also work, but you already configured EVPN in Chapter 3.

CE1 will be a Linux host configured as a BGP route server, CE2 will be a Junos logical system MX. You'll configure the route server and a BGP peering between CE1 and CE2. The logical topology is shown in Figure 4.2.

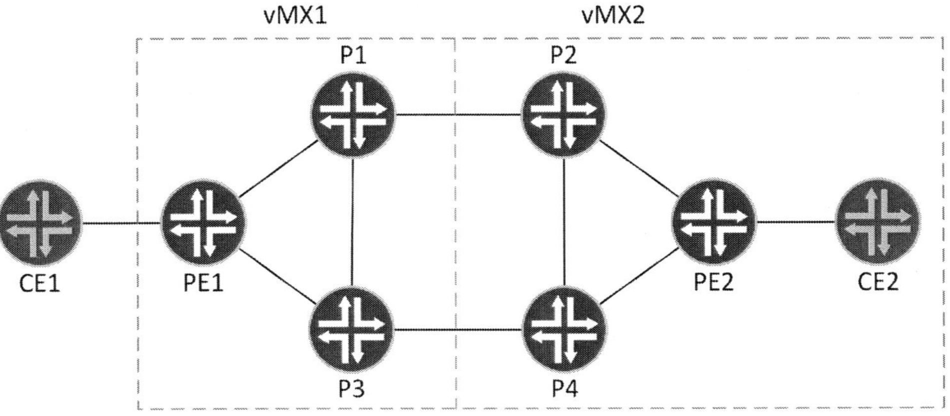

Figure 4.2 Logical Topology

The interface and IP address schema is listed in Table 4.2.

Table 4.2 **Interface and IP Configuration**

Router	Interface	VLAN ID / Peer unit	Connects to	IP address
P1	ge-0/0/3.12	12	P2	192.168.12.1/30
P1	ge-0/0/1.13	13	P3	192.168.13.1/30
P1	ge-0/0/1.15	15	PE1	192.168.15.1/30
P1	Lo0.1			10.1.1.1/32
P2	ge-0/0/3.12	12	P1	192.168.12.2/30
P2	lt-0/0/0.242	244	P4	192.168.24.1/30
P2	lt-0/0/0.262	266	PE2	192.168.26.1/30
P2	Lo0.2			10.2.2.2/32
P3	ge-0/0/2.13	13	P1	192.168.13.2/30
P3	ge-0/0/3.34	34	P4	192.168.34.1/30
P3	ge-0/0/1.35	35	PE1	192.168.35.1/30
P3	Lo0.3			10.3.3.3/32
P4	lt-0/0/0.244	242	P2	192.168.24.2/30
P4	ge-0/0/3.34	34	P3	192.168.34.2/30
P4	lt-0/0/0.464	466	PE2	192.168.46.1/30
P4	Lo0.4			10.4.4.4/32
PE1	ge-0/0/2.15	15	P1	192.168.15.2/30
PE1	ge-0/0/2.35	35	P3	192.168.35.2/30
PE1	ge-0/0/0		CE1	N/A
PE1	Lo0.5			10.5.5.5/32
PE2	lt-0/0/0.266	262	P2	192.168.26.2/30
PE2	lt-0/0/0.466	464	P4	192.168.46.2/30
PE2	lt-0/0/0.686	688	CE2	N/A
PE2	Lo0.6			10.6.6.6/32
CE1	Eth1		PE1	10.0.0.1/24
CE2	lt-0/0/0.688	686	PE2	10.0.0.2/24

Lab vMX Configuration

Base Configuration for the P/PE Core

You will reuse the vMX1 and vMX2 configuration files from the previous chapters. But before getting started, you will need to start both vMX and reset the Junos configuration to factory defaults:

```
root@R1> configure
Entering configuration mode

[edit]
root@R1# load factory-default
warning: activating factory configuration
```

Now that each vMX is at defaults, apply the logical system and IP address configuration as shown in Table 4.2.

Let's configure vMX1 first. On vMX1 the LS routers will be connected together using VLAN tagged interfaces:

1. Set the host name to *vmx1* and configure a password for the root account:

```
set system host-name vmx1
set system root-authentication plain-text-password
```

2. Enable support for VLAN-tagging on ge-0/0/1 through ge-0/0/3:

```
set interfaces ge-0/0/1 flexible-vlan-tagging
set interfaces ge-0/0/2 flexible-vlan-tagging
set interfaces ge-0/0/3 flexible-vlan-tagging
```

3. Create the logical systems. Assign the interfaces and IPs to each P/PE router and enable MPLS support on the interface:

```
set logical-systems P1 interfaces ge-0/0/1 unit 13 vlan-id 13
set logical-systems P1 interfaces ge-0/0/1 unit 13 family inet address 192.168.13.1/30
set logical-systems P1 interfaces ge-0/0/1 unit 13 family mpls
set logical-systems P1 interfaces ge-0/0/1 unit 15 vlan-id 15
set logical-systems P1 interfaces ge-0/0/1 unit 15 family inet address 192.168.15.1/30
set logical-systems P1 interfaces ge-0/0/1 unit 15 family mpls
set logical-systems P1 interfaces ge-0/0/3 unit 12 vlan-id 12
set logical-systems P1 interfaces ge-0/0/3 unit 12 family inet address 192.168.12.1/30
set logical-systems P1 interfaces ge-0/0/3 unit 12 family mpls
set logical-systems P1 interfaces lo0 unit 1 family inet address 10.1.1.1/32
set logical-systems P3 interfaces ge-0/0/1 unit 35 vlan-id 35
set logical-systems P3 interfaces ge-0/0/1 unit 35 family inet address 192.168.35.1/30
set logical-systems P3 interfaces ge-0/0/1 unit 35 family mpls
set logical-systems P3 interfaces ge-0/0/2 unit 13 vlan-id 13
set logical-systems P3 interfaces ge-0/0/2 unit 13 family inet address 192.168.13.2/30
set logical-systems P3 interfaces ge-0/0/2 unit 13 family mpls
set logical-systems P3 interfaces ge-0/0/3 unit 34 vlan-id 34
set logical-systems P3 interfaces ge-0/0/3 unit 34 family inet address 192.168.34.1/30
set logical-systems P3 interfaces ge-0/0/3 unit 34 family mpls
set logical-systems P3 interfaces lo0 unit 3 family inet address 10.3.3.3/32
set logical-systems PE1 interfaces ge-0/0/2 unit 15 vlan-id 15
```

```
set logical-systems PE1 interfaces ge-0/0/2 unit 15 family inet address 192.168.15.2/30
set logical-systems PE1 interfaces ge-0/0/2 unit 15 family mpls
set logical-systems PE1 interfaces ge-0/0/2 unit 35 vlan-id 35
set logical-systems PE1 interfaces ge-0/0/2 unit 35 family inet address 192.168.35.2/30
set logical-systems PE1 interfaces ge-0/0/2 unit 35 family mpls
set logical-systems PE1 interfaces lo0 unit 5 family inet address 10.5.5.5/32
```

Now configure vMX2. On vMX2 the LS routers will be connected using logical tunnel interfaces.

1. Set the host name to *vmx2* and configure a password for the root account:

```
set system host-name vmx2
set system root-authentication plain-text-password
```

2. Enable support for VLAN-tagging on ge-0/0/1 through ge-0/0/3:

```
set interfaces ge-0/0/1 flexible-vlan-tagging
set interfaces ge-0/0/2 flexible-vlan-tagging
set interfaces ge-0/0/3 flexible-vlan-tagging
```

3. Configure FPC slot 0 to support logical tunnel (lt) interfaces. This creates a specific lt interface – make a note of this because you will need it when creating the lt units:

```
set chassis fpc 0 pic 0 tunnel-services
root@vmx2# commit
commit complete

[edit]
root@vmx2# run show interfaces terse | match lt-
lt-0/0/0                up    up
```

4. Create the logical systems. Assign the interfaces and IPs to each P/PE router and enable MPLS support on the interface. The configuration of the lt interface is simple. Create the lt interface and unit. The `peer-unit` specifies the lt `peer-unit` for the far end of the virtual point-to-point link:

```
set logical-systems P2 interfaces ge-0/0/3 unit 12 vlan-id 12
set logical-systems P2 interfaces ge-0/0/3 unit 12 family inet address 192.168.12.2/30
set logical-systems P2 interfaces ge-0/0/3 unit 12 family mpls
set logical-systems P2 interfaces lt-0/0/0 unit 242 encapsulation ethernet
set logical-systems P2 interfaces lt-0/0/0 unit 242 peer-unit 244
set logical-systems P2 interfaces lt-0/0/0 unit 242 family inet address 192.168.24.1/30
set logical-systems P2 interfaces lt-0/0/0 unit 242 family mpls
set logical-systems P2 interfaces lt-0/0/0 unit 262 encapsulation ethernet
set logical-systems P2 interfaces lt-0/0/0 unit 262 peer-unit 266
set logical-systems P2 interfaces lt-0/0/0 unit 262 family inet address 192.168.26.1/30
set logical-systems P2 interfaces lt-0/0/0 unit 262 family mpls
set logical-systems P2 interfaces lo0 unit 2 family inet address 10.2.2.2/32
set logical-systems P4 interfaces ge-0/0/3 unit 34 vlan-id 34
set logical-systems P4 interfaces ge-0/0/3 unit 34 family inet address 192.168.34.2/30
set logical-systems P4 interfaces ge-0/0/3 unit 34 family mpls
set logical-systems P4 interfaces lt-0/0/0 unit 244 encapsulation ethernet
set logical-systems P4 interfaces lt-0/0/0 unit 244 peer-unit 242
set logical-systems P4 interfaces lt-0/0/0 unit 244 family inet address 192.168.24.2/30
set logical-systems P4 interfaces lt-0/0/0 unit 244 family mpls
```

```
set logical-systems P4 interfaces lt-0/0/0 unit 464 encapsulation ethernet
set logical-systems P4 interfaces lt-0/0/0 unit 464 peer-unit 466
set logical-systems P4 interfaces lt-0/0/0 unit 464 family inet address 192.168.46.1/30
set logical-systems P4 interfaces lt-0/0/0 unit 464 family mpls
set logical-systems P4 interfaces lo0 unit 4 family inet address 10.4.4.4/32
set logical-systems PE2 interfaces lt-0/0/0 unit 266 encapsulation ethernet
set logical-systems PE2 interfaces lt-0/0/0 unit 266 peer-unit 262
set logical-systems PE2 interfaces lt-0/0/0 unit 266 family inet address 192.168.26.2/30
set logical-systems PE2 interfaces lt-0/0/0 unit 266 family mpls
set logical-systems PE2 interfaces lt-0/0/0 unit 466 encapsulation ethernet
set logical-systems PE2 interfaces lt-0/0/0 unit 466 peer-unit 464
set logical-systems PE2 interfaces lt-0/0/0 unit 466 family inet address 192.168.46.2/30
set logical-systems PE2 interfaces lt-0/0/0 unit 466 family mpls
set logical-systems PE2 interfaces lo0 unit 6 family inet address 10.6.6.6/32
```

For the routers that are interconnected with lt interfaces you will now be able to verify connectivity between each router with ping. But for routers on vMX1, the Linux bridges and device bindings need to be set up before the logical system routers will be able to communicate.

Virtio Bindings / Linux Bridges

Now let's start to build up the lab starting with the Ethernet connectivity for each vMX as show in Table 4.2. Edit *vmx-junosdev.conf* as follows:

- Create a link between ge-0/0/1 and ge-0/0/2 on vMX1 for the logical system communication.
- Create a link between ge-0/0/3 on vMX1 and ge-0/0/3 on vMX2.
- Create a bridge for the communication between PE1 on vMX1 interface ge-0/0/0 and the Linux route server VM. You will add the Linux VM to the bridge later.

The configuration should be as shown here:

```
interfaces :

     - link_name  : vmx_link_ls
       endpoint_1 :
         - type        : junos_dev
           vm_name     : vmx1
           dev_name    : ge-0/0/1
       endpoint_2 :
         - type        : junos_dev
           vm_name     : vmx1
           dev_name    : ge-0/0/2

     - link_name  : link_vmx_12
       endpoint_1 :
         - type        : junos_dev
           vm_name     : vmx1
           dev_name    : ge-0/0/3
       endpoint_2 :
         - type        : junos_dev
           vm_name     : vmx2
```

```
        dev_name     : ge-0/0/3

    - link_name  : bridge_vmx1_ce1
      endpoint_1 :
        - type        : junos_dev
          vm_name     : vmx1
          dev_name    : ge-0/0/0
      endpoint_2 :
        - type        : bridge_dev
          dev_name    : bridge_vmx1_ce1
```

Now check and then apply the binding configuration. If any of the configuration is already present, but not correct for any reason, the vMX script will fix it. This is useful to know for troubleshooting purposes – if your vMX appears to be fully operational but there is no connectivity, then first check the binding configuration and reapply if necessary:

```
mdinham@vmx-day1:~/vmx-15.1F4-3$ sudo ./vmx.sh --bind-check
Checking package ethtool.........................[OK]
Check Link vmx_link_ls(ge-0.0.1-vmx1, ge-0.0.2-vmx1)
[OK]
Check Link link_vmx_12(ge-0.0.3-vmx1, ge-0.0.3-vmx2)
[Not Present]
Check Bridge port bridge_vmx1_ce1(ge-0.0.0-vmx1)..[Not Present]

mdinham@vmx-day1:~/vmx-15.1F4-3$ sudo ./vmx.sh --bind-dev
Checking package ethtool.........................[OK]
Bind Link vmx_link_ls(ge-0.0.1-vmx1, ge-0.0.2-vmx1)
Warning! Bridge vmx_link_ls already exists
[OK]
Bind Link link_vmx_12(ge-0.0.3-vmx1, ge-0.0.3-vmx2)
[OK]
Bind Bridge port bridge_vmx1_ce1(ge-0.0.0-vmx1)...[OK]
```

Now let's do a quick test of the LS routers on vMX1 and then you will be ready to set up the rest of the lab:

```
root@vmx1> ping logical-system P1 192.168.12.2 rapid
PING 192.168.12.2 (192.168.12.2): 56 data bytes
!!!!!
--- 192.168.12.2 ping statistics ---
5 packets transmitted, 5 packets received, 0% packet loss
round-trip min/avg/max/stddev = 1.940/8.880/31.805/11.577 ms

root@vmx1> ping logical-system P1 192.168.15.2 rapid
PING 192.168.15.2 (192.168.15.2): 56 data bytes
!!!!!
--- 192.168.15.2 ping statistics ---
5 packets transmitted, 5 packets received, 0% packet loss
round-trip min/avg/max/stddev = 2.179/6.928/22.107/7.629 ms
```

Don't forget you can also configure a logical system and run operational mode commands within the context of the logical system by shifting the CLI to the LS router. Notice the prompt changes to show the name of the LS router:

```
root@vmx1> set cli logical-system P3
logical system: P3

root@vmx1:P3> ping 192.168.35.2 rapid
PING 192.168.35.2 (192.168.35.2): 56 data bytes
!!!!!
--- 192.168.35.2 ping statistics ---
5 packets transmitted, 5 packets received, 0% packet loss
round-trip min/avg/max/stddev = 1.694/3.832/9.653/3.088 ms
```

Routing Configuration

OSPF is a popular link-state protocol and enabling it within this lab is a simple process – just configure all links and loopback addresses within area 0. If you would like to test additional OSPF features such as authentication or reference bandwidth, then go ahead. It's also a good idea to set the router-ID on each router to the loopback IP address.

NOTE It's considered best practice to explicitly disable OSPF on the management interfaces, particularly when using "interface all". You don't need to do so here, though, because we are using logical systems and the fxp0 is not present in the logical system.

On vMX1:

```
set logical-systems P1 routing-options router-id 10.1.1.1
set logical-systems P1 protocols ospf area 0.0.0.0 interface all interface-type p2p
set logical-systems P1 protocols ospf area 0.0.0.0 interface lo0.1 passive
set logical-systems P3 routing-options router-id 10.3.3.3
set logical-systems P3 protocols ospf area 0.0.0.0 interface all interface-type p2p
set logical-systems P3 protocols ospf area 0.0.0.0 interface lo0.3 passive
set logical-systems PE1 routing-options router-id 10.5.5.5
set logical-systems PE1 protocols ospf area 0.0.0.0 interface all interface-type p2p
set logical-systems PE1 protocols ospf area 0.0.0.0 interface lo0.5 passive
```

On vMX2:

```
set logical-systems P2 routing-options router-id 10.2.2.2
set logical-systems P2 protocols ospf area 0.0.0.0 interface all interface-type p2p
set logical-systems P2 protocols ospf area 0.0.0.0 interface lo0.2 passive
set logical-systems P4 routing-options router-id 10.4.4.4
set logical-systems P4 protocols ospf area 0.0.0.0 interface all interface-type p2p
set logical-systems P4 protocols ospf area 0.0.0.0 interface lo0.4 passive
set logical-systems PE2 routing-options router-id 10.6.6.6
set logical-systems PE2 protocols ospf area 0.0.0.0 interface all interface-type p2p
set logical-systems PE2 protocols ospf area 0.0.0.0 interface lo0.6 passive
```

Don't forget to verify that the OSPF neighbors are fully established. Each PE router should have two neighbors and each P router should have three neighbors:

```
root@vmx1> show ospf neighbor logical-system P1
Address          Interface              State     ID               Pri  Dead
192.168.13.2     ge-0/0/1.13            Full      10.3.3.3         128    34
192.168.15.2     ge-0/0/1.15            Full      10.5.5.5         128    34
192.168.12.2     ge-0/0/3.12            Full      10.2.2.2         128    36

root@vmx1> show ospf neighbor logical-system P3
Address          Interface              State     ID               Pri  Dead
192.168.35.2     ge-0/0/1.35            Full      10.5.5.5         128    34
192.168.13.1     ge-0/0/2.13            Full      10.1.1.1         128    33
192.168.34.2     ge-0/0/3.34            Full      10.4.4.4         128    32

root@vmx1> show ospf neighbor logical-system PE1
Address          Interface              State     ID               Pri  Dead
192.168.15.1     ge-0/0/2.15            Full      10.1.1.1         128    34
192.168.35.1     ge-0/0/2.35            Full      10.3.3.3         128    36

root@vmx2> show ospf neighbor logical-system P2
Address          Interface              State     ID               Pri  Dead
192.168.12.1     ge-0/0/3.12            Full      10.1.1.1         128    38
192.168.24.2     lt-0/0/0.242           Full      10.4.4.4         128    39
192.168.26.2     lt-0/0/0.262           Full      10.6.6.6         128    30

root@vmx2> show ospf neighbor logical-system P4
Address          Interface              State     ID               Pri  Dead
192.168.34.1     ge-0/0/3.34            Full      10.3.3.3         128    39
192.168.24.1     lt-0/0/0.244           Full      10.2.2.2         128    33
192.168.46.2     lt-0/0/0.464           Full      10.6.6.6         128    39

root@vmx2> show ospf neighbor logical-system PE2
Address          Interface              State     ID               Pri  Dead
192.168.26.1     lt-0/0/0.266           Full      10.2.2.2         128    35
192.168.46.1     lt-0/0/0.466           Full      10.4.4.4         128    35
```

You could also run the command `show ospf neighbor logical-system all` to show the neighbors for all logical system routers with just one CLI command.

Spend a few moments here checking routing tables and running ping tests to be sure that each router has full reachability to the rest of the network.

MPLS Configuration

You have already enabled the MPLS family on the router-to-router interfaces, so all that needs to be done here is to enable the RSVP and MPLS protocols on each router and to set up an LSP between PE1 and PE2. Specify the interfaces individually, if you prefer.

On vMX1:

```
set logical-systems P1 protocols rsvp interface all
set logical-systems P1 protocols mpls interface all
set logical-systems P3 protocols rsvp interface all
set logical-systems P3 protocols mpls interface all
set logical-systems PE1 protocols rsvp interface all
set logical-systems PE1 protocols mpls interface all
```

On vMX2:

```
set logical-systems P2 protocols rsvp interface all
set logical-systems P2 protocols mpls interface all
set logical-systems P4 protocols rsvp interface all
set logical-systems P4 protocols mpls interface all
set logical-systems PE2 protocols rsvp interface all
set logical-systems PE2 protocols mpls interface all
```

Now let's build the LSP between PE1 and PE2. Remember that an LSP is unidirectional, so the configuration must be applied on both PE1 and PE2.

On vMX1:

```
set logical-systems PE1 protocols mpls label-switched-path to-PE2 to 10.6.6.6
set logical-systems PE1 protocols mpls label-switched-path to-PE2 no-cspf
```

On vMX2:

```
set logical-systems PE2 protocols mpls label-switched-path to-PE1 to 10.5.5.5
set logical-systems PE2 protocols mpls label-switched-path to-PE1 no-cspf
```

Make sure that you verify that the LSP has established correctly. If for some reason the LSP is down, then use the `extensive` option to look for the reason. Perhaps the destination is missing from the route table, or MPLS is not enabled on an interface (`family mpls` or `protocol mpls`):

```
root@vmx2> show mpls lsp logical-system PE2
Ingress LSP: 1 sessions
To              From            State Rt P     ActivePath       LSPname
10.5.5.5        10.6.6.6        Up     0 *                      to-PE1
Total 1 displayed, Up 1, Down 0

Egress LSP: 1 sessions
To              From            State   Rt Style Labelin Labelout LSPname
10.6.6.6        10.5.5.5        Up       0  1 FF       3        - to-PE2
Total 1 displayed, Up 1, Down 0

Transit LSP: 0 sessions
Total 0 displayed, Up 0, Down 0
```

Adding Another Non-vMX Virtual Machine

Now let's build a Linux VM and configure it to be a BGP route server using ExaBGP software. A useful addition to any lab!

Build a Linux VM with virsh

Let's build the Linux VM.

1. Download Ubuntu directly to your home directory on the the KVM host:

```
mdinham@vmx-day1:~/vmx-15.1F4-3$ cd
mdinham@vmx-day1:~$ wget http://archive.ubuntu.com/ubuntu/dists/trusty/main/installer-
amd64/current/images/netboot/mini.iso
```

2. You may need install the "virtinst"package. This is a CLI tool to create a new VM:

```
mdinham@vmx-day1:~$ sudo apt-get install virtinst
```

3. Create a directory to store your VM disk images:

```
mdinham@vmx-day1:~$ mkdir VMs
```

4. Build the VM using the `virt-install` tool. This tool will create the VM configuration files and spawn a VNC server for you to connect to:

```
mdinham@vmx-day1:~$ sudo virt-install --virt-type kvm --name linux-
day1 --ram 512 --cdrom mini.iso --disk VMs/linux-day1.img,size=2 --network bridge=br-
ext --network bridge=bridge_vmx1_ce1 --os-type=linux --os-
variant=ubuntutrusty --graphics vnc,listen=0.0.0.0,port=5910 --noautoconsole
```

Most of these command-line options are self-explanatory:

- Network configuration – there are two interfaces added to the host so that you can SSH to the VM. The eth0 interface is connecting to the management interface bridge (`br-ext`) also used by the vMX, and the second interface connects to the PE1_CE1 bridge that was created earlier.
- Graphics configuration – VNC is used to complete the installation and is configured here to listen on port 5910.

5. Load up your VNC client and connect to the IP address of the KVM host on port 5910. The VNC window will take you to the Ubuntu installer screen. Select eth0 as the primary interface and then progress through the installer as you did during Chapter 2.

6. After a short wait the installation will complete and the system will reboot.

Connect to Linux VM

After installation, check that the new VM is running. This is done using virsh. Notice the `--all` option to show domains that are not running. If the `--all` is not specified, then only information on running domains is shown:

```
mdinham@vmx-day1:~$ sudo virsh list --all
 Id    Name                           State
----------------------------------------------------
 2     vcp-vmx1                       running
 3     vfp-vmx1                       running
 5     vcp-vmx2                       running
 6     vfp-vmx2                       running
 -     linux-day1                     shut off
```

Here you can see the vMX VMs are running but the new Linux VM `linux-day1` is shut off. It's time to get it started up:

```
mdinham@vmx-day1:~$ sudo virsh start linux-day1
Domain linux-day1 started

mdinham@vmx-day1:~$ sudo virsh list --all
 Id    Name                           State
----------------------------------------------------
 2     vcp-vmx1                       running
 3     vfp-vmx1                       running
 5     vcp-vmx2                       running
 6     vfp-vmx2                       running
 20    linux-day1                     running
```

You can now connect back to the VM with VNC. If you prefer to be able to SSH directly in to the VM, connect to the CLI with VNC and install *openssh server*:

```
mdinham@linux-day1: ~$ sudo apt-get install openssh-server
```

Once the SSH service has been installed you can SSH to the IP address assigned to the VM interface eth0. This interface will be using DHCP unless you prefer to change the configuration to be statically assigned. The command `ifconfig eth0` can be used to find out the IP address to use for SSH.

To complete the build of this Linux CE1 it is now necessary to configure the CE1-PE1 interface. Use the IP addressing as shown in Table 4.2.

Connect to CE1 via SSH or VNC and modify the configuration of eth1:

```
mdinham@linux-day1:~$ cd /etc/network/
mdinham@linux-day1:/etc/network$ sudo vi interfaces
```

Update the interfaces configuration:

```
auto eth1
iface eth1 inet static
address 10.0.0.1
network 255.255.255.0
```

And bring up the interface:

```
mdinham@linux-day1:/etc/network$ sudo ifup eth1
```

The build of CE1 is now complete!

Check the VM to vMX bridges

The installer will have automatically connected the VM interfaces to the correct bridges. If you need to check that everything is correct, or make changes manually, this can be done with the following steps.

Use virsh to show you which interfaces on the VM are mapped to the Linux Bridges. Here you can see vnet0 is assigned to br-ext and vnet1 to bridge_vmx1_ce1:

```
mdinham@vmx-day1:~$ sudo virsh domiflist linux-day1
Interface  Type       Source     Model       MAC
-------------------------------------------------------
vnet0      bridge     br-ext     virtio      52:54:00:bb:a4:77
vnet1      bridge     bridge_vmx1_ce1 virtio      52:54:00:69:99:e2
```

The same thing can be seen by looking at the bridges directly:

```
mdinham@vmx-day1:~$ brctl show br-ext
bridge name     bridge id               STP enabled     interfaces
br-ext           8000.000c29510c44        yes              br-ext-nic
                                                          eth0
                                                          vcp_ext-vmx1
                                                          vcp_ext-vmx2
                                                          vfp_ext-vmx1
                                                          vfp_ext-vmx2
                                                          vnet0

mdinham@vmx-day1:~$ brctl show bridge_vmx1_ce1
bridge name     bridge id               STP enabled     interfaces
bridge_vmx1_ce1 8000.fe060a0efff0       no               ge-0.0.0-vmx1
                                                         vnet1
```

As expected, the correct VM interface has been assigned to each bridge. If the VM interfaces have been assigned to the default bridge, they can easily be corrected by deleting the interface from the bridge, and then reassigning it to a new bridge, like this:

```
mdinham@vmx-day1:~$ sudo brctl delif virbr0 vnet1
mdinham@vmx-day1:~$ sudo brctl addif bridge_vmx1_ce1 vnet1
```

Putting It All Together

A Virtual Private LAN service (VPLS) appears to connected CE devices as an Ethernet LAN. This is accomplished by the VPLS incorporating LAN-like functionality such as MAC learning, flooding, and forwarding across an MPLS network.

VPLS Configuration

VPLS is defined in two different RFCs – RCF4761 (*BGP Auto-Discovery and Signaling for VPLS*) and RFC4762 (*Virtual Private LAN Service over LDP*). In this lab you will be configuring LDP-signaled VPLS.

To complete the VPLS configuration, as you are using LDP signaled VPLS, LDP must be enabled on the loopback interface of each PE. The VPLS configuration itself is done within a routing instance.

NOTE There is no auto-discovery with LDP-signaled VPLS so when you configure the PE routers you will need to specify every neighbor PE that is participating in the VPLS. This static neighbor configuration with LDP signaled VPLS is one reason why BGP signaled VPLS would scale better in a large network, but LDP signaled is fine for this lab.

1. Enable LDP on the PE loopback interfaces. Remember PE1 is running on vMX1 and PE2 is running on vMX2:

```
set logical-systems PE1 protocols ldp interface lo0.5

set logical-systems PE2 protocols ldp interface lo0.6
```

2. Create router CE2 as a logical system router on vMX2 and add the point-to-point link between CE2 and PE2:

```
set logical-systems CE2 interfaces lt-0/0/0 unit 688 encapsulation ethernet
set logical-systems CE2 interfaces lt-0/0/0 unit 688 peer-unit 686
set logical-systems CE2 interfaces lt-0/0/0 unit 688 family inet address 10.0.0.2/24

set logical-systems PE2 interfaces lt-0/0/0 unit 686 encapsulation ethernet-vpls
set logical-systems PE2 interfaces lt-0/0/0 unit 686 peer-unit 688
```

3. Configure the VPLS routing instances. On PE1 the VPLS interface is the Ethernet interface facing CE1 (ge-0/0/0). Since you are only using VPLS on the interface, it's okay to use an encapsulation of `ethernet-vpls` rather than `flexible-ethernet-services`:

On vMX1:

```
set interfaces ge-0/0/0 encapsulation ethernet-vpls
set logical-systems PE1 interfaces ge-0/0/0 unit 0
set logical-systems PE1 routing-instances VPLS instance-type vpls
set logical-systems PE1 routing-instances VPLS interface ge-0/0/0.0
set logical-systems PE1 routing-instances VPLS protocols vpls vpls-id 1
set logical-systems PE1 routing-instances VPLS protocols vpls neighbor 10.6.6.6
```

4. Create the VPLS on PE2. This time the VPLS interface isn't a Gigabit interface, it is the lt interface on PE2 that connects to CE2, so be sure to set the encapsulation to `ethernet-vpls` rather than `ethernet`. Being able to use a lt interface with VPLS is another reason that they are so flexible!

On vMX2:

```
set logical-systems PE2 interfaces lt-0/0/0 unit 686 encapsulation ethernet-vpls
set logical-systems PE2 routing-instances VPLS instance-type vpls
set logical-systems PE2 routing-instances VPLS interface lt-0/0/0.686
set logical-systems PE2 routing-instances VPLS protocols vpls vpls-id 1
set logical-systems PE2 routing-instances VPLS protocols vpls neighbor 10.5.5.5
```

5. Verification – check that VPLS has been established on PE1 and PE2:

```
root@vmx2> show vpls connections logical-system PE2
Layer-2 VPN connections:

Legend for connection status (St)
EI -- encapsulation invalid      NC -- interface encapsulation not CCC/TCC/VPLS
EM -- encapsulation mismatch     WE -- interface and instance encaps not same
VC-Dn -- Virtual circuit down    NP -- interface hardware not present
CM -- control-word mismatch      -> -- only outbound connection is up
CN -- circuit not provisioned    <- -- only inbound connection is up
OR -- out of range               Up -- operational
OL -- no outgoing label          Dn -- down
LD -- local site signaled down   CF -- call admission control failure
RD -- remote site signaled down  SC -- local and remote site ID collision
LN -- local site not designated  LM -- local site ID not minimum designated
RN -- remote site not designated RM -- remote site ID not minimum designated
XX -- unknown connection status  IL -- no incoming label
MM -- MTU mismatch               MI -- Mesh-Group ID not available
BK -- Backup connection          ST -- Standby connection
PF -- Profile parse failure      PB -- Profile busy
RS -- remote site standby  SN -- Static Neighbor
LB -- Local site not best-site   RB -- Remote site not best-site
VM -- VLAN ID mismatch

Legend for interface status
Up -- operational
Dn -- down

Instance: VPLS
  VPLS-id: 1
    Neighbor                   Type  St     Time last up          # Up trans
    10.5.5.5(vpls-id 1)        rmt   Up     Feb 23 16:21:22 2016           1
      Remote PE: 10.5.5.5, Negotiated control-word: No
      Incoming label: 800000, Outgoing label: 800000
      Negotiated PW status TLV: No
      Local interface: vt-0/0/10.51380224, Status: Up, Encapsulation: ETHERNET
        Description: Intf - vpls VPLS neighbor 10.5.5.5 vpls-id 1
      Flow Label Transmit: No, Flow Label Receive: No

root@vmx1> show vpls connections logical-system PE1
Layer-2 VPN connections:

Legend for connection status (St)
EI -- encapsulation invalid      NC -- interface encapsulation not CCC/TCC/VPLS
EM -- encapsulation mismatch     WE -- interface and instance encaps not same
VC-Dn -- Virtual circuit down    NP -- interface hardware not present
CM -- control-word mismatch      -> -- only outbound connection is up
CN -- circuit not provisioned    <- -- only inbound connection is up
```

```
OR -- out of range             Up -- operational
OL -- no outgoing label        Dn -- down
LD -- local site signaled down   CF -- call admission control failure
RD -- remote site signaled down  SC -- local and remote site ID collision
LN -- local site not designated  LM -- local site ID not minimum designated
RN -- remote site not designated RM -- remote site ID not minimum designated
XX -- unknown connection status  IL -- no incoming label
MM -- MTU mismatch             MI -- Mesh-Group ID not available
BK -- Backup connection        ST -- Standby connection
PF -- Profile parse failure    PB -- Profile busy
RS -- remote site standby  SN -- Static Neighbor
LB -- Local site not best-site   RB -- Remote site not best-site
VM -- VLAN ID mismatch

Legend for interface status
Up -- operational
Dn -- down

Instance: VPLS
  VPLS-id: 1
    Neighbor                  Type  St     Time last up          # Up trans
    10.6.6.6(vpls-id 1)       rmt   NP
```

Here you can see that the VPLS is up on PE2, but PE1 is showing an error "interface hardware not present". Remember that PE2 is using lt interfaces and so has been configured with `tunnel-services`, but PE1 has not. VPLS requires that tunnel services be configured, or for a router without tunnel services the `no-tunnel-services` statement will create a label-switched interface (LSI) to enable the VPLS functionality to work. Let's use `no-tunnel-services` so you can see the difference. Add the following to vMX1:

```
set logical-systems PE1 routing-instances VPLS protocols vpls no-tunnel-services

root@vmx1> show vpls connections logical-system PE1
Layer-2 VPN connections:

Legend for connection status (St)
EI -- encapsulation invalid      NC -- interface encapsulation not CCC/TCC/VPLS
EM -- encapsulation mismatch     WE -- interface and instance encaps not same
VC-Dn -- Virtual circuit down    NP -- interface hardware not present
CM -- control-word mismatch      -> -- only outbound connection is up
CN -- circuit not provisioned    <- -- only inbound connection is up
OR -- out of range               Up -- operational
OL -- no outgoing label          Dn -- down
LD -- local site signaled down   CF -- call admission control failure
RD -- remote site signaled down  SC -- local and remote site ID collision
LN -- local site not designated  LM -- local site ID not minimum designated
RN -- remote site not designated RM -- remote site ID not minimum designated
XX -- unknown connection status  IL -- no incoming label
MM -- MTU mismatch               MI -- Mesh-Group ID not available
BK -- Backup connection          ST -- Standby connection
PF -- Profile parse failure      PB -- Profile busy
RS -- remote site standby  SN -- Static Neighbor
LB -- Local site not best-site   RB -- Remote site not best-site
VM -- VLAN ID mismatch

Legend for interface status
Up -- operational
Dn -- down

Instance: VPLS
  VPLS-id: 1
    Neighbor                  Type  St     Time last up          # Up trans
    10.6.6.6(vpls-id 1)       rmt   Up     Feb 23 16:27:44 2016           1
```

```
Remote PE: 10.6.6.6, Negotiated control-word: No
Incoming label: 262145, Outgoing label: 800000
Negotiated PW status TLV: No
Local interface: lsi.17825792, Status: Up, Encapsulation: ETHERNET
  Description: Intf - vpls VPLS neighbor 10.6.6.6 vpls-id 1
Flow Label Transmit: No, Flow Label Receive: No
```

Great - the VPLS on PE1 is now up. Notice the LSI local interface on PE1 compared with the VT local interface on PE2.

At this point the VPLS configuration is complete and you should have direct connectivity between CE1 and CE2. Now, let's configure the BGP peering between CE1 and CE2. Let's first check that everything is okay using a quick ping across the VPLS:

```
root@vmx2> ping logical-system CE2 10.0.0.1 rapid
PING 10.0.0.1 (10.0.0.1): 56 data bytes
!!!!!
--- 10.0.0.1 ping statistics ---
5 packets transmitted, 5 packets received, 0% packet loss
round-trip min/avg/max/stddev = 2.798/3.071/3.536/0.269 ms

mdinham@linux-day1:/etc/network$ ping 10.0.0.2
PING 10.0.0.2 (10.0.0.2) 56(84) bytes of data.
64 bytes from 10.0.0.2: icmp_seq=1 ttl=64 time=2.64 ms
64 bytes from 10.0.0.2: icmp_seq=2 ttl=64 time=1.79 ms
^C
--- 10.0.0.2 ping statistics ---
2 packets transmitted, 2 received, 0% packet loss, time 1002ms
rtt min/avg/max/mdev = 1.790/2.216/2.642/0.426 ms
```

Try It Yourself: BGP Signaled VPLS

See what you can learn about BGP and VPLS by configuring BGP signaled VPLS instead of LDP signaled VPLS.

- Configure BGP between PE1 and PE2
- Enable the `l2vpn signaling` address family
- Create VPLS routing instances and assign CE interfaces
- Verify CE connectivity

Route Server Configuration

The final step in this *Day One* book is to configure a BGP peering between CE1 and CE2. The reason for using a Linux server running ExaBGP is because it provides you with flexibility in BGP announcements.

In this book's case, CE2 will simulate a peering router, in other words, it will be configured to advertise eBGP routing information, and iBGP will be configured between CE1 and CE2.

For the route server, use the ExaBGP software. It is available from https://github.com/Exa-Networks/exabgp. Connect to the CE VM and use wget to download ExaBGP:

```
mdinham@linux-day1:~$ wget https://github.com/Exa-Networks/exabgp/archive/3.4.10.tar.gz
```

Extract ExaBGP and create a simple configuration file called *day1.conf*:

```
mdinham@linux-day1:~$ tar -xzf 3.4.10.tar.gz
mdinham@linux-day1:~$ cd exabgp-3.4.10/
mdinham@linux-day1:~/exabgp-3.4.10$
mdinham@linux-day1:~/exabgp-3.4.10$ vi day1.conf
```

Set up the configuration file as shown next. The options should be self explanatory. It's a very simple file, but as you can see the tool is quite flexible. There is also an API to allow more advanced route advertisement functionality. ExaBGP is a powerful tool, and this configuration is just a subset of what is possible:

```
group internal {
    hold-time 180;
    local-as 65000;
    peer-as 65000;
    router-id 10.0.0.1;

    static {
        route 10.10.10.0/24 next-hop 10.0.0.1 as-path [ 10 ] ;
        route 10.10.20.0/24 next-hop 10.0.0.1 as-path [ 10 20 ] ;
        route 10.10.30.0/24 next-hop 10.0.0.1 as-path [ 10 20 30 ] ;
        route 10.10.40.0/24 next-hop 10.0.0.1 as-path [ 40 50 60 ] ;
        route 10.10.50.0/24 next-hop 10.0.0.1 as-path [ 70 80 90 ] ;
        route 10.10.60.0/24 next-hop 10.0.0.1 as-path [ 100 120 130 ] ;
        route 10.10.70.0/24 next-hop 10.0.0.1 as-path [ 140 150 160 ] ;
        route 10.10.80.0/24 next-hop 10.0.0.1 as-path [ 170 180 ] ;
    }

    neighbor 10.0.0.2 {
        local-address 10.0.0.1;
    }
}
```

Start ExaBGP with this command – it will run in the foreground:

```
mdinham@linux-day1:~/exabgp-3.4.10$ sbin/exabgp day1.conf
```

Finally, configure a BGP neighbor on CE2:

```
set logical-systems CE2 protocols bgp local-as 65000
set logical-systems CE2 protocols bgp group internal type internal
set logical-systems CE2 protocols bgp group internal peer-as 65000
set logical-systems CE2 protocols bgp group internal neighbor 10.0.0.1
```

With ExaBGP running, the session will come up, and you will see the BGP routes being received:

```
root@vmx2> show route logical-system CE2
```

```
inet.0: 10 destinations, 10 routes (10 active, 0 holddown, 0 hidden)
+ = Active Route, - = Last Active, * = Both

10.0.0.0/24        *[Direct/0] 01:44:38
                    > via lt-0/0/0.688
10.0.0.2/32        *[Local/0] 01:44:38
                      Local via lt-0/0/0.688
10.10.10.0/24      *[BGP/170] 00:01:07, localpref 100
                      AS path: 10 I, validation-state: unverified
                    > to 10.0.0.1 via lt-0/0/0.688
10.10.20.0/24      *[BGP/170] 00:01:07, localpref 100
                      AS path: 10 20 I, validation-state: unverified
                    > to 10.0.0.1 via lt-0/0/0.688
10.10.30.0/24      *[BGP/170] 00:01:07, localpref 100
                      AS path: 10 20 30 I, validation-state: unverified
                    > to 10.0.0.1 via lt-0/0/0.688
10.10.40.0/24      *[BGP/170] 00:01:07, localpref 100
                      AS path: 40 50 60 I, validation-state: unverified
                    > to 10.0.0.1 via lt-0/0/0.688
10.10.50.0/24      *[BGP/170] 00:01:07, localpref 100
                      AS path: 70 80 90 I, validation-state: unverified
                    > to 10.0.0.1 via lt-0/0/0.688
10.10.60.0/24      *[BGP/170] 00:01:07, localpref 100
                      AS path: 100 120 130 I, validation-state: unverified
                    > to 10.0.0.1 via lt-0/0/0.688
10.10.70.0/24      *[BGP/170] 00:01:07, localpref 100
                      AS path: 140 150 160 I, validation-state: unverified
                    > to 10.0.0.1 via lt-0/0/0.688
10.10.80.0/24      *[BGP/170] 00:01:07, localpref 100
                      AS path: 170 180 I, validation-state: unverified
                    > to 10.0.0.1 via lt-0/0/0.688
```

At this point you have a working VPLS environment and BGP running directly across the VPLS between the two CE devices. You could further modify the BGP configuration on CE2 to include BGP policy, and adjust the route announcements on CE1 to validate your policy is working correctly.

Try It Yourself: Expand the Environment Further

You have now built a flexible lab environment – why not try to expand it further? Add another PE router device to the lab, and add a third CE router to the VPLS. Try to configure MPLS VPNs rather than VPLS and add the three CE routers to the VPN. You are only limited by your imagination!

Summary

In this chapter you discovered how simple it is to scale your lab environment to a multi-router topology with multiple vMXs and logical systems. Large lab topologies can easily be created and the powerful feature set of vMX allows you to test many different protocols and topologies. Now that you've built this environment – expand it further on your own and have fun learning!

Chapter 5

Troubleshooting the vMX

This chapter highlights a few more ways to troubleshoot vMX operation. Generally speaking, you can accomplish most things on vMX with Juniper's vmx.sh orchestration script, but just in case things are not going entirely to plan, here are a few more troubleshooting tips for you to try out.

Verify vMX VM state

To verify the VMs you can use libvirt's `virsh list` command. This will display the name and state of the vMX VMs on your KVM hosts. The state can be: *running, idle, paused, shutdown, crashed, or dying.*

Use the following commands to start and stop VMs, but ideally you will use the vmx.sh script to manage this process.

- `virsh destroy`—Force stop a VM (but does not delete the VM)
- `virsh start`—Start an inactive VM.

VCP and VFP Communication

If you run `the show interfaces terse` command on the VCP and you do not see any ge-0/0/x interfaces listed, then it is possible that the connection between VCP and VFP has not established or that the VFP has not booted up correctly.

On your first attempt to log in to the VFP console, if you do not get a response (i.e. the console appears to have locked) then it is possible that the VFP has not booted up.

To check for VFP errors during boot up:

Start the vMX using the orchestration script. As soon as the VFP boots, then be ready to console in to the VFP:

```
./vmx.sh -console vfp vmx1
```

Look for any error messages or kernel panic during boot. For example, if you see "`Kernel panic - not syncing: Attempted to kill init! exitcode=0x0000000b`" then go and check that your BIOS settings are correct.

If VFP has booted correctly and you see a login prompt on the console (`login with the default username root / password root`), look for syslog entries containing the RPIO or HOSTIF messages:

```
RPIO: Accepted connection from 172.16.0.1:50896 <-> vPFE:3000
RPIO: Accepted connection from 172.16.0.1:56098 <-> vPFE:3000
HOSTIF: Accepted connection
```

If the VCP cannot connect to the VFP, and the VFP syslog file does not display the RPIO and HOSTIF messages, you should follow the next few procedures:

1. Run the `request chassis fpc slot 0 restart` command from the VCP CLI. If an FPC is in transition, and an error message is displayed, then run `restart chassis-control`.

2. If these commands do not correct the problem, check to see if you can ping the VFP from the VCP `routing-instance __juniper_private1__` via the internal bridge:

```
root> ping 128.0.0.16 routing-instance __juniper_private1__
PING 128.0.0.16 (128.0.0.16): 56 data bytes
64 bytes from 128.0.0.16: icmp_seq=0 ttl=64 time=0.273 ms
64 bytes from 128.0.0.16: icmp_seq=1 ttl=64 time=0.606 ms
```

NOTE The IP addresses that are automatically assigned to the em1 interface on the VCP and internal interface on the VFP vary between Junos release 14.1 and 15.1:

```
14.1 -  VCP 172.16.0.1, VFP 172.16.0.2
15.1 -  VCP 128.0.0.1, VFP 128.0.0.16
```

If you still have problems, then perform these additional steps:

1. Check that the Linux bridge configuration is correct. Run `brctl show` from the KVM host shell and check the internal bridge configuration.

2. Using virsh, check that both VMs are actually running. Run `sudo virsh -c qemu:///system list`

3. Restart the FPC from the VCP VM. Run `request chassis fpc restart`

4. Restart the chassis management process from VCP VM. Run `restart chassis-control`

5. Stop and start the VFP VM.

6. Stop and start the VCP VM.

7. Restart the KVM host.

If completion of all the above steps has not helped, then it's time for you to talk to JTAC, or post on Juniper's J-Net forums.

VFP Log Files

If you wish to look at the forwarding plane log files, they can be found in the following locations:

- Log files, as usual for Linux these are located in /var/log
- Crash logs can be found in /var/crash

Virtio Troubleshooting

If the VCP and VFP are operational but you have lost connectivity between vMX instances on the same host, or from a vMX instance to external devices, then the first place to start looking (if you are using virtio interfaces) is the Linux bridges on the KVM host. You can check these out yourself, or use the vmx.sh script to check for you.

To check the Linux bridges yourself, run `brctl show` on the host and check that the correct bridges are present, and that all the interfaces you expect to see have been added to the bridges. Remember the interfaces could be a combination of vMX instance virtual interfaces and KVM host physical interfaces.

If you are using the vmx.sh script to check the bridges, then follow this troubleshooting procedure.

If you want to see a working set of bridges:

```
mdinham@vmx-day1:~$ sudo brctl show
bridge name     bridge id               STP enabled     interfaces
br-ext          8000.000c29510c44       yes             br-ext-nic
                                                        eth0
                                                        vcp_ext-vmx1
                                                        vcp_ext-vmx2
                                                        vfp_ext-vmx1
                                                        vfp_ext-vmx2
br-int-vmx1             8000.525400a2025e       yes     br-int-vmx1-nic
                                                        vcp_int-vmx1
                                                        vfp_int-vmx1
```

```
br-int-vmx2              8000.525400de027d      yes     br-int-vmx2-nic
                                                        vcp_int-vmx2
                                                        vfp_int-vmx2
bridge_vmx12             8000.fe060a0efff7      no      ge-0.0.3-vmx2
virbr0                   8000.fe060a0efff0      yes     ge-0.0.0-vmx1
                                                        ge-0.0.0-vmx2
vmx2_link_ls             8000.fe060a0efff5      no      ge-0.0.1-vmx2
                                                        ge-0.0.2-vmx2
vmx_link_ls              8000.fe060a0efff1      no      ge-0.0.1-vmx1
                                                        ge-0.0.2-vmx1
```

If you run `./vmx.sh --bind-check` the script will tell you if everything is configured correctly:

```
mdinham@vmx-day1:~/vmx-15.1F4-3$ ./vmx.sh --bind-check
Checking package ethtool..........................[OK]
Check Link vmx_link_ls(ge-0.0.1-vmx1, ge-0.0.2-vmx1)
[OK]
Check Link vmx2_link_ls(ge-0.0.1-vmx2, ge-0.0.2-vmx2)
[OK]
Check Bridge port bridge_vmx12(ge-0.0.3-vmx1).....[OK]
Check Bridge port bridge_vmx12(ge-0.0.3-vmx2).....[OK]
```

As you can see here, everything looks good. Now what would happen if you were to delete one of the vMX interfaces from a bridge:

```
mdinham@vmx-day1:~/vmx-15.1F4-3$ sudo brctl delif bridge_vmx12 ge-0.0.3-vmx1
mdinham@vmx-day1:~/vmx-15.1F4-3$ ./vmx.sh --bind-check
Checking package ethtool..........................[OK]
Check Link vmx_link_ls(ge-0.0.1-vmx1, ge-0.0.2-vmx1)
[OK]
Check Link vmx2_link_ls(ge-0.0.1-vmx2, ge-0.0.2-vmx2)
[OK]
Check Bridge port bridge_vmx12(ge-0.0.3-vmx1).....[Misconfigured]
Check Bridge port bridge_vmx12(ge-0.0.3-vmx2).....[OK]
```

You can see how the script has reported back that the bridge is misconfigured because ge-0/0/3 on vMX1 is missing from the bridge. This is easily fixed by re-running vmx.sh with the `--bind-dev` option:

```
mdinham@vmx-day1:~/vmx-15.1F4-3$ sudo ./vmx.sh --bind-dev
Checking package ethtool..........................[OK]
Bind Link vmx_link_ls(ge-0.0.1-vmx1, ge-0.0.2-vmx1)
Warning! Bridge vmx_link_ls already exists
[OK]
Bind Link vmx2_link_ls(ge-0.0.1-vmx2, ge-0.0.2-vmx2)
Warning! Bridge vmx2_link_ls already exists
[OK]
Bind Bridge port bridge_vmx12(ge-0.0.3-vmx1)......[OK]
Bind Bridge port bridge_vmx12(ge-0.0.3-vmx2)......[OK]

mdinham@vmx-day1:~/vmx-15.1F4-3$ brctl show bridge_vmx12
bridge name     bridge id               STP enabled     interfaces
bridge_vmx12            8000.fe060a0efff3       no      ge-0.0.3-vmx1
                                                        ge-0.0.3-vmx2
```

As you can see here, the vMX script has corrected the error for you.

If during a vMX start operation you receive an error like the one shown here, and the vMX will not start, this is probably due to the the vMX VMs not being stopped by the orchestration script. Perhaps the physical host was rebooted without the vMX being shut down.

```
==================================================
    System Setup Completed
==================================================
Generate libvirt files...........................[OK]
Sleep 2 secs.....................................[OK]
Find configured management interface.............eth0
Find existing management gateway.................br-ext
Check if eth0 is already enslaved to br-ext.......[Yes]
Create br-int-vmx2...............................[Failed]
error: Failed to define network from /home/mdinham/vmx-15.1F4-3/build/vmx2/xml/br-int-generated.xml
error: operation failed: network 'br-int-vmx2' already exists with uuid 96aa825b-5f02-48ca-bbb4-135b6a7e89ce
Log file........................................../dev/null
==================================================
 Aborted!. 1 error(s) and 0 warning(s)
==================================================
```

To correct this issue, you can run the orchestration script with the `--stop` option to tidy things up and then try the `--start` again. Don't run the `--cleanup` option because this will clean up all information about the vMX instance including your Junos configuration!

Book End Summary

Now you've learned how to build and configure vMX, why not go ahead and deploy the vMX router to meet your own specific requirements? The vMX supports the DCI and Layer 2/Layer 3 technologies that are available on the physical MX and if a feature becomes available on MX, it will push down to vMX. Perhaps the virtual MX router will enable you to quickly introduce a new service or sandbox test a new configuration.

Here are some examples of use cases for vMX:

- Service Provider Edge – a virtual MPLS PE in scale out deployment scenarios, or as a peering router.
- Data Center Gateway – a gateway router that is capable of supporting the different DC overlay, DC interconnect, and L2 technologies used in the DC such as GRE, VXLAN, VPLS, and EVPN.

- Enterprise WAN router – an Internet gateway or for proving an overlay network over a service providers MPLS or Layer 2 network.
- Virtual Route Reflector.
- Virtual Broadband Network Gateway (vBNG) within Service Provider infrastructure.
- In your lab environment to allow you do do network simulation and configuration testing.

MORE? For case studies and a deep dive on the architecture of vMX, see *Juniper MX Series, 2nd Edition – O'Reilly Media:* http://shop.oreilly.com/product/0636920042709.do.

Let's now review what you've accomplished by reading this *Day One* book. You built a Ubuntu KVM host and then configured an instance of vMX in a simple lab topology. This topology was then scaled up from a simple four router topology to a topology consisting of eight routers that could be easily scaled to thirty routers and beyond. Some cool features of Junos were configured – such as VPLS and EVPN.

At this point why not try to scale the topology further – go ahead and add more routers, and perhaps learn about a different protocol – you could take the final topology and remove OSPF, but using IS-IS as the IGP instead?

You now have a working MPLS installation, so why not get more familiar with it? Add a few more P routers, and maybe play with Traffic Engineering LSPs and force traffic over a particular path. But most importantly - get familiar with troubleshooting Junos on the lab topology.

The topology you built can now be extended to support even the most complicated JNCIE configuration, so it's time to go ahead with vMX on your own. Have fun deploying vMX in your own environment!

If you would like to know more about features of the Junos OS that can be configured on your vMX, then check out other the *Day One* books at http://www.juniper.net/dayone.

Appendix

Getting Started with vMX on VMware

Although this book has focused on the KVM release of vMX, there is a VMware release also available. This Appendix shows you how to install vMX on VMware, starting with the installation of the ESXi hypervisor.

Once you have installed vMX then be sure to go ahead and walk through all of the lab exercises shown here on your VMware build of vMX.

ESXi Installation

Let's get started with the installation of ESXi. As with the KVM build I'm doing this running ESXi as a nested virtual machine on a MacBook, but the process will be the same if you are doing it on bare metal.

If you don't already have an ISO image of VMware then Register with VMware and download the ESXi ISO from https://my.vmware.com/web/vmware/evalcenter?p=free-esxi6.

Once you have downloaded the ISO image, boot your machine directly from the ISO. The installation of ESXi is a simple process. Go through the installation steps one by one and reboot ESXi once the installation has completed.

Following the reboot, ESXi will load up and if your management LAN is running DHCP the ESXi host will have already been assigned an IP address for management. You will now need to download the VMware client to be able to manage ESXi free. Open a web browser and connect to the ESXi IP – download the tools as suggested, and then load up the client.

Once the client is loaded, first you should license the ESXi host. You can get a free license from VMware at the ESXi download page: https://my.vmware.com/group/vmware/evalcenter?p=free-esxi6.

In the web client, the license is applied at Home – Inventory – click *configuration* and then *Licensed Features*. You can then click *Edit* to add the license.

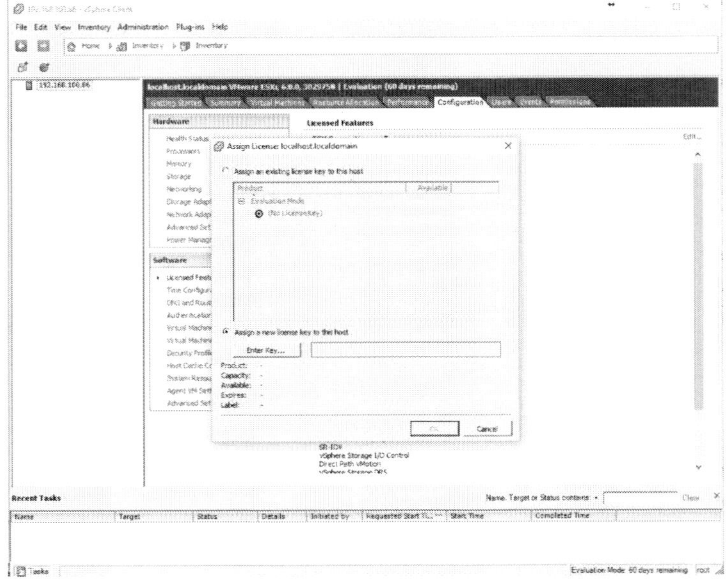

vMX Installation

If you have a valid login, you can download vMX directly from the vMX download page: https://www.juniper.net/support/downloads/?p=vmx#sw.

Once you have downloaded the vMX software, next load up the client for your ESXi server and login.

ALERT! Be sure to check the latest install and operating guides for your version of vMX. It is a vibrant technology and Juniper is making improvements to vMX every calendar quarter. At the time of this writing, the process to install vMX on VMware is as documented here, however, there will soon be an OVA template installer. Depending on when you read these pages, the VMware installation process might be very different than what's been written.

Copy Files to the Datastore

Before progressing any further you will need to extract the vMX package. All of the vmdk files are located in the subdirectory "/vmdk". The content of the VMware package is as shown here:

- Software image for vMX VCP: `jinstall64-vmx-15.1F4.15-domestic.vmdk`
- Software image for VCP file storage: `vmxhdd.vmdk`
- Software image for VFP: `vFPC-20151203.vmdk`

Virtual hard disk with bootstrapping information: `metadata_usb.vmdk`. This is used by the VCP to store configuration data.

Once the the files have been extracted, return to the VMware client and click the summary tab. Select the appropriate Datastore under Storage, right click, and select *Browse Datastore*.

Now create a folder called "vmx" and then click the upload file button and upload all of the vmdk files listed above to this new folder.

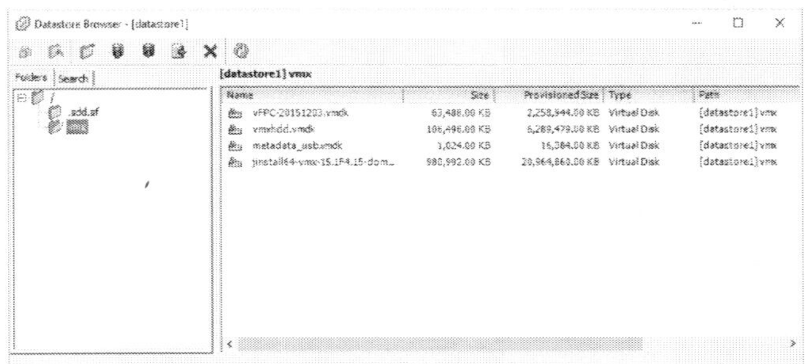

Set Up the vMX Network

The VMware release is no different than the KVM release when it comes to the required default networks. There are a minimum of three networks that will need to be configured:

- Management network (br-ext)
- Internal network for VCP and VFP communication (br-int)
- Data interfaces

To create these networks, go back to the ESXi client, select the ESXi server, and click the Configuration tab. Select Networking under Hardware. In the top right corner click *Add networking*.

Create each of the three required networks.

Management Network

The management network is created by following the steps listed here:

Select Virtual Machine as the connection type and click Next.

Select Use vSwitch0 and click Next.

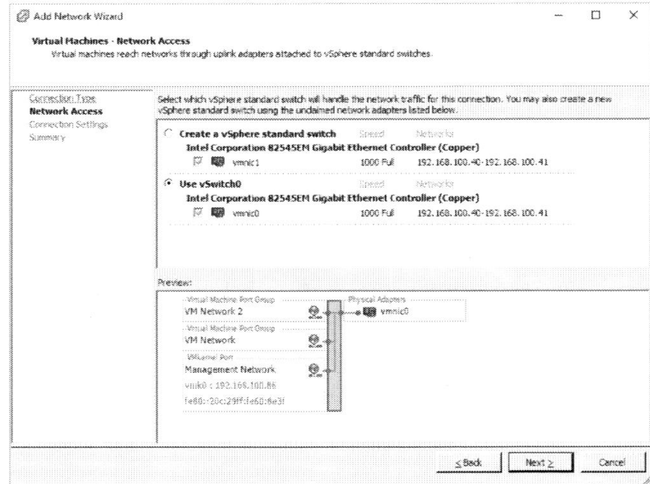

At port group properties, set network label to *br-ext* and click the Next button.

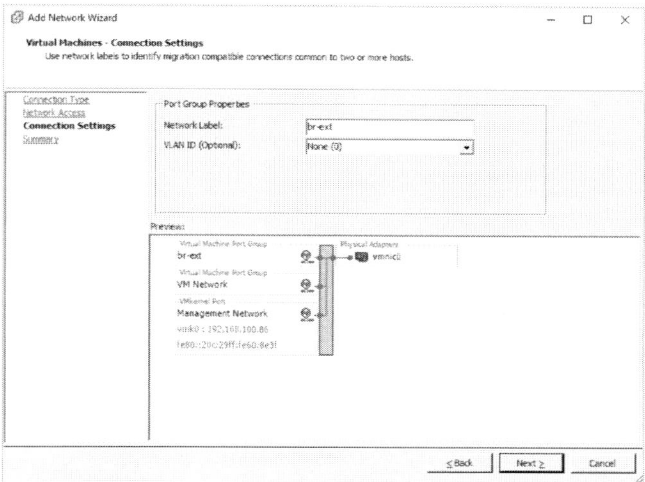

Now click finish. You will see the new port group "br-ext" has been added to the standard switch vSwitch0.

Internal Network

The internal network is used only for communication between the VCP and VFP and is created by following these steps. A separate internal network is required for each vMX instance.

Select Networking under Hardware. In the top right corner click *Add networking*. Select Virtual Machine as the connection type and click Next.

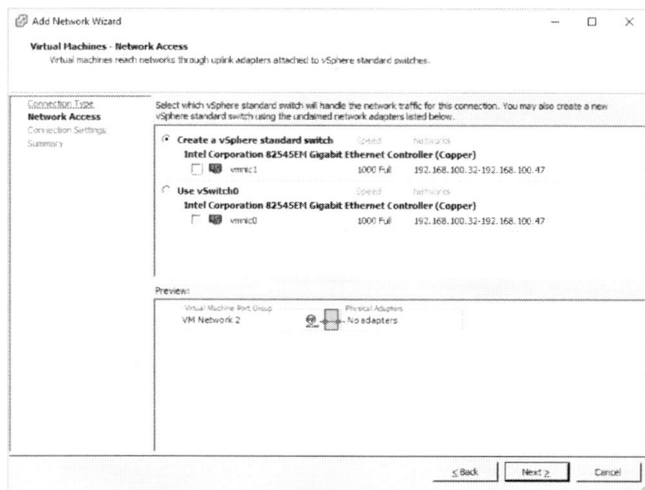

This time select Create a vSphere standard switch and clear all physical NIC check boxes, then click next. This vSwitch is only going to be used for communication between the VCP and VFP, which is why no physical NIC is assigned.

For network label, use *br-int-<identifier>, e.g br-int-vmx1.*

You should now have a port group called "br-int-vmx1", with no adapters assigned.

Data Network

Now you will need to add a data network. This process is repeated according to the number of data NICs that you wish to add.

Let's create a single adapter named *p1p1*.

Again, select Networking under Hardware. In the top right corner click Add networking.

Select Virtual Machine as the connection type and click next.

Select Create a vSphere standard switch and add the physical NIC that you want to use, and click next.

Name the connection *p1p1*, click Next, and finish.

Now repeat the above steps if you have any more data adapters to add to vMX.

NOTE If you would like to join two vMXs together on the same VMware system, then simply repeat the above steps to create another vSwitch. You do not need to add any physical NICs to the vSwitch (this is the same configuration as the Internal vSwitch). Then add the VFP data interface for each vMX to this vSwitch. The process to setup the VFP interfaces is below.

Complete the network configuration

You will now see the three networks in the networking summary screen – br-ext, br-int, and p1p1.

You must enable promiscuous mode in all vSwitches so that packets with any MAC addresses can reach the vMX. This configuration is needed for OSPF to work properly.

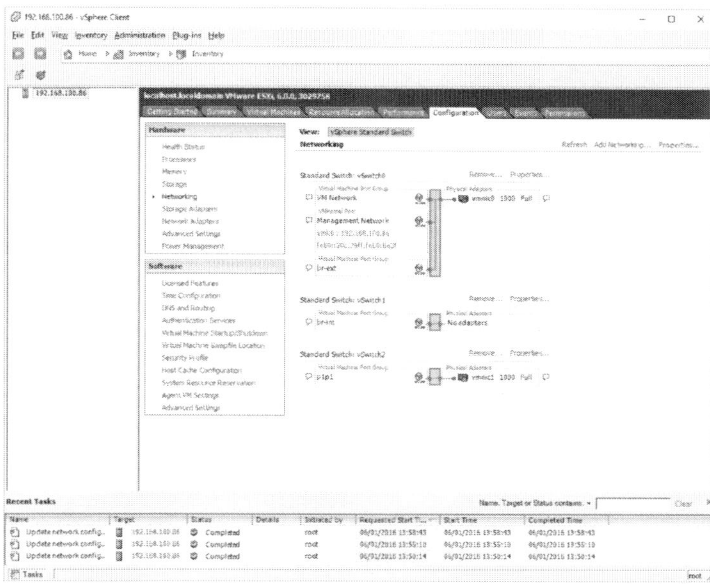

For each vSwitch, click properties, then select vSwitch and click Edit. Select security and change promiscuous mode to accept.

Set Up the vMX Virtual Machines

Just like vMX on KVM, there are two VMs that must be created – the VCP running the Junos OS, and the VFP running an x86 virtualized release of Trio running on Wind River Linux.

The process for creating both of the VMs is very similar. It's a simple case of following the VMware wizard and choosing the correct settings for the VM.

Let's get started with the VCP.

VCP

Here are the steps required to create the VCP virtual machine:

1. Within the VMware client, select the ESXi host, right click, new virtual machine.

2. Select to create a custom VM, and click Next.

3. Give the machine a suitable name, for example: *vcp-vmx1*.

4. Select the datastore where you would like to store the VM and click Next.

5. Set the VM version to 8.

6. For the guest OS type, choose Other, Other (64-bit).

7. Select one virtual socket, and one CPU core per socket, to assign a total of one CPU core to the VCP.

8.Provision 2GB of memory.

9. In the network setup, select two network adapters.

10. Assign br-ext as the first adapter and br-int as the second adapter.

11. Set both NICs to be e1000.

12. Select LSI Logic Parallel as the SCSI controller.

13. When prompted to select the disk type, choose use an existing virtual disk, and then on the next screen browse to the correct datastore and select the `jinstall64-vmx-15.1F4.15-domestic.vmdk` image that you uploaded earlier.

14. At the advanced options page, simply click next.

15. Select to edit the virtual machine settings before completion and click continue.

16. Now you need to add two more hard drives – click Add, and then Hard Disk, this time selecting `vmxhdd.vmdk` as the second drive.

17. Repeat the add Hard Disk process again, this time adding the `metadata_usb.vmdk` image as the third drive.

NOTE This third hard drive is important – if you don't configure it then the first time VCP boots, VCP will set up as an "olive" not vMX!

You can now boot the VCP - if the boot process appears to wait at "Loading /boot/loader" do not worry, on the VMware release you don't see the full Junos OS boot process on the console.

VFP

The process for creating the VFP is similar. The process below outlines the steps required to create the VFP VM.

1. Within the VMware client, select the ESXi hosts, right click, *new virtual machine*.

2. Select custom and press next.

3. Give the machine a suitable name, for example: *vfp-vmx1*.

4. Select the datastore where you would like to store the VM and press next.

5. Set the VM version to 8.

6. For the guest OS, choose Other, Other (64-bit).

7. When prompted to select the number of CPUs, for this build the minimum you can choose is three virtual sockets, and one CPU core per socket, to give a total of three CPU cores assigned to the VCP.

8. Provision 8GB of memory.

9. In the network setup, select at least three network adapters, assigning br-ext as the first adapter and br-int as the second adapter. Set them both to be e1000 adapters. The data adapters that you configured earlier can now be added, set them to be vmxnet3 or e1000 depending on your preference. For better performance, I'd suggest you use vmxnet3 because this is a paravirtualization adapter.

10. Select LSI Logic Parallel as the SCSI controller.

11. When prompted to select the disk to use, choose use an existing virtual disk, and then on the next screen browse to the datastore and select the `vFPC-20151203.vmdk` image that you uploaded earlier (bear in mind the image naming has changed from vPFE* to vFPC* in this latest release of vMX).

12. At the advanced options page, simply click Next.

13. At Ready to Complete, you can click Finish and boot the VFP.

NOTE On my installation, the Juniper supplied image needed to be converted from sparse to thin or thick provisioned using vmkfstools, otherwise the VM refused to boot (I was getting a VMware error related to free space even though the drives were not full). You may only have to do this if using ESXi 6 rather than the recommended release ESXi 5.5.

Serial Console

To aid with the troubleshooting and configuration of vMX on VMware you should now set up a serial port connection to each VM so you can connect to the serial console of the VCP and VFP. This is accomplished by redirecting a telnet session to the serial port on the VM and is configured on VMware like this:

1. Your vMX VMs will need to be stopped before you can complete all of these steps, so if you have not already done so then stop both VMs now.

2. In the VMware client. Select the ESXi server and then the configuration tab.

3. Select Security Profile and click Properties next to Firewall.

4. Tick the box "VM serial port connected over network" and click OK. This setting will open up the ESXi firewall to allow the traffic.

5. Now you can add the serial port to each vMX VM. In the left plane, select the VCP VM and right-click then select Edit Settings. The VM Properties will display, and now click Add to bring up the Add Hardware Wizard.

6. From the list of devices choose Serial Port, and click Next.

7. For Port Type, choose Connect via Network, and click Next.

8. In Network Backing, select Server and specify Port URI in the format `telnet://:port-number`. For example, if you wish to use port 8601 for the serial connection on the VCP then you would type `telnet://:8601` in to the Port URI box. Make sure that Connect at power on is selected, and click Next.

9. Click Finish.

Repeat steps 5 through 9 for the VFP VM, this time choosing a different port number in step 8, and then restart both VMs.

You can now use telnet to access the VCP or VFP serial ports by connecting to the telnet port specified in step 8 above.

NOTE Be aware that your VMware license may not permit you to use remote serial ports.

Verification

At this point if both machines have powered on successfully you should have a running vMX.

Now load the VCP VM console, log in, and run the Junos OS command `show chassis fpc`. After a few moments you should see the FPC as online and ge-* interfaces will appear.

Now that you have built vMX on VMware, it's time to return to Chapter 3 and go through the EVPN lab exercise.